The Gospel of Jesus of Nazareth

PETER GILLIES

The Gospel of Jesus of Nazareth

A freethinking, scriptural look at
Jesus of Nazareth
& the Son of Man's singular mission
to free Israel from its tribal God

A·B·C·

abceditions

enjoy life & love others
be you & have fun

All rights reserved, including the right of translation into foreign languages. No part of this work may be reproduced, stored in a retrieval system, distributed or transmitted in any form or by any means – be it electronic, mechanical, photocopying, recording, or otherwise – without the prior written permission of the publisher, except in the case of brief quotations embodied in critical reviews and certain other uses as permitted by copyright law.

A·B·C· EDITIONS ♦ FRANCE

Copyright © 2015 by Peter Gillies
All rights reserved
The moral right of the author has been asserted

The Gospel of Jesus of Nazareth
ISBN 978-2-9546352-3-1

PUBLISHED IN THE UNITED KINGDOM

♦ ♦ ♦ ♦ ♦ ♦ ♦

To my children
…with love

Preface

WHILE I AM not, properly speaking, a classicist, a majority of the verses comprising *The Gospel of Jesus of Nazareth* have been crafted to reflect the original Greek wording of the Gospels. That said, this is first and foremost a work of interpretation, one that stems from my subjective appreciation of the biblical Scriptures. It is in no way a foray into the complex world of textual criticism and it does not presume to be definitive in its approach.

Likewise, I am not a biblical scholar. However, I have been pondering Jesus of Nazareth for some forty-odd years and asking myself the same questions, time and again: Who was he? What was he trying to do? What happened to his corpse after his death?

Unless better evidence comes to light one day in the future, the four canonical Gospels will remain our principal historical source for insights into the life, aims and teachings of Jesus of Nazareth. In my quest to discern the man behind the Christian myth that imbues the Gospels, I have come to feel that the true challenge presented to us by Jesus is neither his supposed divinity nor his miraculous works, but rather this: how are we to make sense of what must be seen as a keystone of his teachings — that he was to give his life on behalf of many, and that his followers must partake of his flesh and blood — within the context of Judaism, which had never ceased to condemn human sacrifice and to forbid the eating of blood?

If the Last Supper occurred as it is related in the Gospels, then Jesus was initiating his disciples into a symbolic violation of Mosaic Law that would have rightfully led to their being forever cut off from the Chosen People. This, coupled with the reports that Jesus portrayed his imminent death as being a sacrifice willed by Yhwh — *"Abba, Father, all things are possible to you. Please remove this cup from me. However, not what I desire, but what you desire."* — should suggest to us that Jesus was seeking to induce a profound spiritual crisis in the lives of his disciples. For if the Jewish tribal God, so vehemently opposed to human sacrifice, were to tacitly accept the sacrificial death of an innocent Jewish son, then did he not transgress his own Law? And if certain members of his Chosen People, with patent disregard for his statutes, were to willfully engage in the symbolic eating of blood and human flesh, then was this not an unbrookable act of defiance? Jesus' design seems calculated both to sow seeds of doubt about their tribal God in the hearts of his Jewish followers and to force Yhwh's hand.

To explore these ideas, *The Gospel of Jesus of Nazareth* risks an admittedly unorthodox approach by presenting itself in the guise of Scripture. The text's reasoning is developed primarily through the straightforward use of cross reference, and the reader is invited to ponder the compelling implications that may be drawn from the juxtaposition of significant biblical verses. A substratum of further argumentation is advanced through the inclusion of two passages from the Hebrew Scriptures (from Isaiah and from Ezekiel) and — although it plays but a minor role — through the infrequent yet judicious alteration of certain words and verses. With regard to the latter, it is worth keeping in mind that the Bible has always been subject to change: the Scriptures have undergone revision, verses and even entire passages have been added or excised, and words that convey one sense have been replaced by others to convey a different sense as various groups have striven to insure that the sacred texts both underpin their dogmas and reflect their vision of the truth. We may presume that similar modifications occurred in the oral traditions and written accounts that are thought to have preceded and informed the Gospels, as those who had personally known and followed Jesus and newer members of the then nascent Jesus-movement sought to make sense of his life and crucifixion. With that as a premise, in a handful of instances *The Gospel of Jesus of Nazareth* takes historical license by extrapolating backwards from the extant Gospel manuscripts to imagine 'antecedent' readings for certain passages — readings that we would understand as having been gradually suppressed by the early Christian church prior to the redaction of the Gospels, and so 'lost' to history. The reader would be mistaken, though, to infer that I am somehow seeking by this to covertly rewrite the Scriptures, or to falsify the historical record; rather, the purpose of these fictitious readings is to focus attention on certain incongruities that are found in the authentic Gospel manuscripts and to offer what I think are plausible suggestions for how we might clarify those passages, or account for the readings that have come down to us.

Regardless of whether we hew to the strict confines of academic scholarship or permit ourselves – as I have done here – to speculate with greater latitude, our efforts to decipher Jesus' true intentions will always fall within the realm of conjecture, hampered as they are by the insufficiencies of the historical record and the utter dearth of primary sources. Though we try to unravel the Gordian knot, the man from Galilee remains elusively hidden in its deeper folds. For what it is worth, *The Gospel of Jesus of Nazareth* is my freethinking attempt to cut straight through to the heart of the mystery.

Introduction

JESUS OF NAZARETH abides as one of history's most enigmatic figures.

The Gospel accounts that have come down to us leave much unsaid, and the details that they do give are often sketchy. While it is possible that Jesus studied the Scriptures as a youth, it is perhaps more probable that he was untutored. It appears that he became a follower of John the Baptist for a short time; then he left John and went his own way. Leaving Nazareth for reasons unknown to us, he came to settle in Capernaum, on the northern shores of the Sea of Galilee, and it was there in the last year (or years) of his life that everything coalesced. Jesus began to teach his own spiritual message – first locally, then further afield. He spoke as one 'having authority'; his words rang true; and although certain teachings caused many of his followers to withdraw, still people listened, and some were especially devoted to him.

But Jesus came with more than just a spiritual message. He came with a mission: to free the house of Israel from bondage. This notion necessarily raises the question: by whom, or what, were the Jews enslaved? It is my view that Jesus came to regard the Jewish people as being enslaved by YHWH, the tribal God of Israel – and it was to secure the liberation of his coreligionists from their everlasting covenant with YHWH that Jesus gave his life.*

To convey Jesus and his intentions in this light, *The Gospel of Jesus of Nazareth* advances a carefully wrought interpretation, one whose reasoning is elucidated by the scriptural verses cited in the margins. Certain salient aspects are worth noting:

ᶓ *The Gospel of Jesus of Nazareth* opens with a passage from Ezekiel. Here, the prophetic Scriptures pertaining to the downfall of the rulers of Tyre and Babylon are linked via margin notes to the God of Israel. I suggest that Jesus could have read in these prophesies a veiled promise of YHWH's ouster and Israel's liberation.

ᶓ Jesus is understood to be human, not the divine son of God. Nevertheless, like all Jews – *"Israel is my son, my firstborn"* – Jesus is a son of YHWH. The story of the Lord's angel visiting Mary serves both to underscore this notion in allegorical fashion and to elevate Jesus to a special position with regard to Israel's tribal God. This in turn dictates the implications of his death on the cross.

ᶓ In the story of Jesus being tempted in the wilderness, a scriptural correlation between YHWH and Satan is set forth.

ᶓ Certain miracles are narrated in such a way as to suggest from what grain of truth each story may have grown.

---

* We may note that if this were indeed Jesus' intent, he would have been no less guilty of having *'enticed Israel to apostasy'* than the Yeshu mentioned in the Babylonian Talmud, *Tractate Sanhedrin*, 43a.

INTRODUCTION

> ❧ Here identified as *'the disciple whom Jesus loved'*, Judas is cast in a positive light. Whereas Christians have vilified him for two millennia, I am persuaded that Judas, entrusted with the paramount mission of betraying Jesus' person to the Jewish authorities, was not only Jesus' closest confidant, but the one disciple to whom he may have fully revealed his intentions.

> ❧ In his trial before the Sanhedrin, Jesus is accused of blasphemy not because he has claimed to be the Son of God, but because he has pronounced the Sacred Name.

> ❧ The Gospel accounts of Jesus appearing in resurrected form are omitted. Instead, in a scripturally supported interpretation, it is here understood that following Jesus' death on the cross, certain unnamed individuals conveyed his corpse from the tomb in Jerusalem to a designated mountain in Galilee. There, exposed to the sky, and in accordance with numerous scriptural prophesies, it would have been eaten by vultures and wild animals.

Jesus chose for his death to coincide with the Passover festival commemorating Israel's release from slavery in Egypt, and it is within this context that *The Gospel of Jesus of Nazareth* construes his intentions. As quoted in Leviticus, the God of Israel declares, *'For the sons of Israel are my slaves [* עבדי *]; they are my slaves, whom I brought out from the land of Egypt. I, Y*HWH*, am your god.'* Seen in this light, Jesus' statement *'and the truth shall set you free'* takes on the very meaning his interlocutors understood when they objected, *'We are the descendants of Abraham's seed, and have never been enslaved by anyone.'* In my view, Jesus felt otherwise. Having concluded an *'everlasting covenant'* with Abraham, Yhwh considered Israel to be his *'own possession'*, *'a kingdom of priests and a holy nation.'* Though he threatened the Jews with dire consequences should they disobey his statutes, still he would not release them from the Mosaic covenant.

Even so, certain sins were inexpiable, and — if committed intentionally — would result in a Jew being cut off from his people. The eating of blood, expressly forbidden, was of this sort. Consider then that Jesus insisted he was to *'give his life as a ransom for many'* and that his followers must partake of his blood. For a Jew, such apostasy was unthinkable: human sacrifice and the eating of blood were an abomination before Yhwh. Consequently, any Jew who deliberately adhered to Jesus' teachings would be cut off from Israel — in a word, 'freed' from the covenant.

It is my opinion that Jesus was seeking neither to found a new religion nor to reform Judaism, but rather to set in motion, through his sacrificial death on the cross, the irrevocable abrogation of the Mosaic covenant. Anticipating that Yhwh himself would not fail to punish such rebellious apostasy by returning to inflict the terrible eschatological retributions that had been promised through the prophets, Jesus forewarned his followers about the tribulations that were sure to come. *'Most certainly I say to you, this generation will not pass away until all these things happen,'* he told them. *'But when these things begin to happen, straighten yourselves up, and lift up your heads, because your redemption draws near.'*

INTRODUCTION

Once they were released from their bondage to Yhwh, his fellow Jews could at last enter into what Jesus understood to be the true kingdom of God. This was not some earthly kingdom to come, as pledged by Yhwh and foretold by the prophets. Rather, Jesus taught his followers that the kingdom of God was within them… and that they need only welcome it, in the same way as one receives a child.

However, Jesus also warned that *'many will come in my name'*, who would lead many astray. Indeed, many did – and one in particular. Though a contemporary of Jesus, he never once heard the Galilean speak, nor did he ever walk with him. Yet Saul of Tarsus, who came to be known as the Apostle Paul, established a new religion in Jesus' name. To that end, he not only recast the Galilean's message and teachings, but he changed the man's name as well. Jesus of Nazareth, as he was originally known to his friends and followers, would be henceforth known instead by the name that Paul so fervently bestowed upon him: *Iésous Christos*.

The Gospel of Jesus of Nazareth

*Y*OU *shall place these words of mine upon your heart and your soul, you shall bind them as a sign upon your hand, and as a frontlet between your eyes.*

Deuteronomy 11:18

*A*ND *he causes all, the small and the great, the rich and the poor, the free and the slaves, to receive a mark upon their right hand, or upon their foreheads.*

Revelation 13:16

The Gospel of Jesus of Nazareth

THE beginning of the gospel of Jesus of Nazareth, the son of man.

2 As it is written in Ezekiel the prophet, "SON OF MAN, SAY TO THE PRINCE OF TYRE, 'THUS SAYS THE LORD GOD:[a]

3 YOUR HEART IS PROUD, AND YOU SAY, "I AM GOD,[b] SITTING ON A GOD'S THRONE[c] IN THE MIDST OF THE OPEN SEAS."[d]

4 "'BUT YOU ARE ONLY A MAN,[e] THOUGH YOU BOAST YOURSELF TO BE LIKE GOD.[f]

5 "'YOU ARE WISER THAN DANIEL, FOR THERE ARE NO SECRETS THAT YOU DO NOT KNOW,[g] AND YOU HAVE USED YOUR WISDOM AND YOUR UNDERSTANDING TO AMASS RICHES;[h] YOUR WISDOM HAS MADE YOU WEALTHY, AND PROUD.[i]

a Eze 28:2
b Isa 44:6
   Isa 45:11,12
   Isa 46:9
   Isa 47:10
   Isa 54:5
c Ex 25:17-22
   2Sa 6:2
   Ps 99:1
   Isa 6:1-3
   Eze 10:1
   Eze 43:7
d Eze 28:2
e Ge 32:24,28,30
   Eze 1:26
   Eze 43:6
f De 32:39
   Isa 41:4
   Isa 43:13
   Eze 28:2,9
g Job 38:1-41
   Job 39:1-30
   Job 40:6-24
   Job 41:1-34
   Eze 28:3
h Ex 25:1-9
   Ex 38:24-29
   Jos 6:19
   1Ch 29:2-9
   Hag 2:8
i 1Ch 29:11
   Eze 28:5
   Da 4:35

Prologue

6 "'You were sealing a pattern of perfection;[j] full of wisdom were you,[k] and perfect in beauty.[l]

7 "'You were in Eden,[m] the garden of God; every precious stone was your covering,[n] and the gold of your settings, fine workmanship, was in you.[o] The day you were created, they were prepared.[p]

8 "'You were the anointed cherub who covers.[q] On the holy mountain of God,[r] you walked in the midst of the stones of fire.[s]

9 "'You were perfect in your ways from the day you were created, until wrong was found in you.[t]

10 "'But your heart was filled with pride[u] because of your beauty,[v] and your wisdom was corrupted for the sake of your splendor.[w] Your riches filled you with violence, and you sinned.[x]

11 "'Therefore, I will cast you down from the mountain of God,[y]

12 And I will destroy you, O covering cherub, from the midst of the stones of fire.[z]

The angel of the Lord comes to Mary

13 "'ONTO THE EARTH I WILL THROW YOU.[a] I SHALL BRING FORTH A FIRE FROM THE MIDST OF YOU, IT SHALL DEVOUR YOU;[b] AND I WILL BRING YOU TO ASHES UPON THE EARTH, IN THE SIGHT OF ALL.[c]

14 "'AND THEY THAT KNOW YOU WILL BE ASTONISHED, AND YOU WILL BE NO MORE.'"[d]

15 Now the angel[e] of *the* Lord came to a city of Galilee, whose name *was* Nazareth,[f]

16 to a [1]virgin *who was* betrothed to a man whose name was [2]Joseph, of *the* house of David; and the name of the [1]virgin *was* [3]Mary.[g]

17 And having come to her, he said, "Rejoice, *you who are* favored with grace. The Lord *is* with you!"[h]

18 And at the word, she was greatly agitated, and was debating what kind of salutation this might be.[i]

19 And the angel said to her, "Fear not, Mary – you have indeed found favor with God.[j]

20 "And behold, you will conceive in your womb and will bring forth a son, and you will call his name [4]Jesus."[k]

---

1 Or, *maiden*
2 Gr., *Iósēph*, for the Hebrew *Yosef*
3 Gr., *María*, for the Hebrew *Miriam*
4 Gr., *Iēsous*, for the Hebrew *Yehoshua'*, or Joshua

x Ex 20:13
　Ex 23:7
　De 19:10
　Ps 109:16
　Pr 28:17
　La 2:11-13
　La 2:20-22
　La 4:4,9-11
　Eze 28:16
　Mr 14:36
　Mr 15:34
y Eze 28:16
　Jn 12:31
z Eze 28:16
a Isa 14:12
　Eze 28:17
b Jer 51:25
c Eze 28:18
d Isa 14:16,17
　Isa 47:11
　Jer 10:11
　Jer 51:26
　Eze 28:19
e Ge 32:24,26,28
　Ho 12:3,4
f Lu 1:26
g Lu 1:27
h Ge 32:29,30
　Lu 1:28
i La 3:38
　Lu 1:29
j Lu 1:30
k Lu 1:31

Joseph desires to divorce Mary secretly

l *Lu 1:34*
m *De 22:23,24*
   Isa 14:14
n *Ps 2:7*
   Ps 82:6
   Eze 28:2
   Lu 1:35
o *Le 19:20*
p *Ps 51:5*
   Lu 1:38
q *Lu 1:38*
r *Mt 1:18*
s *De 22:13-21*
t *Mt 1:19*
u *Mt 1:20*
v *Job 4:12,13*

21 But Mary said to the angel, "How will this be, since I know not a man?"[l]

22 And answering, the angel said to her, "Holy spirit will come upon you, and power of *the* highest will overshadow you,[m] wherefore the holy *spirit* being born will be called *a* son of God."[n]

23 But Mary said, "Behold, the female slave[o] of the Lord – be it done to me according to your word."[p]

24 And the angel departed from her.[q]

25 Now the birth of Jesus was thus – his mother Mary having been betrothed to Joseph, but before their coming together, was found to be pregnant.[r]

26 But Joseph, her husband, being righteous, and not wishing to make her an example,[s] desired [5]to send her away secretly.[t]

27 But he having considered this, *the* angel of *the* Lord appeared to him in a dream, saying, "Joseph, son of David, fear not to receive Mary as your wife, for the *child* in her, having been conceived from spirit, is holy."[u]

28 But Joseph, having been woken from sleep,[v] did as the angel of the Lord commanded him, and

---
5 Or, *to divorce*

Jesus is born

received his wife,^w

29 and knew her not until she had given birth to her firstborn son.^x

30 And when *the* eight days were fulfilled for his circumcision,^y his name was called Jesus, the *name he had* been called by the angel before his being conceived in the womb.^z

31 And when the days of their purification^a were fulfilled, they brought him to Jerusalem, to present *him* to the Lord,^b

32 and to offer a sacrifice according to the law of the Lord — two young pigeons.^c

33 And when they had accomplished everything according to the law of the Lord, they returned to Galilee, to their city, Nazareth.^d

34 And the child grew and became strong, being filled with wisdom, and God's grace was upon him.^e

35 And every year, his parents went to Jerusalem at the feast of the Passover.^f

36 And when he was twelve years *old*, they had gone up, according to the custom of the feast.^g

37 And having completed the days, as they were returning, the boy Jesus remained behind in

w Mt 1:24
x Mt 1:25
y Ge 17:10-14
  Ex 22:29,30
  Le 12:2,3
z Lu 2:21
a Le 12:4
b Ex 13:2,12-15
  Nu 3:13
  Lu 2:22
c Le 12:6-8
  Lu 2:24
d Lu 2:39
e Lu 2:40
f Ex 23:15
  De 16:1-6
  Lu 2:41
g Lu 2:42

Jerusalem; and his parents did not know it.[h]

38 But having assumed him to be in their caravan, they went a day's journey; and they searched for him among the relatives and the acquaintances,[i]

39 and not having found *him*, they returned to Jerusalem, searching for him.[j]

40 And it came about, after three days, *that* they found him in the temple, sitting in the midst of the teachers, and hearing them and questioning them.[k]

41 And having seen him, they were thunderstruck, and his mother said to him, "Child! Why have you done this to us? Behold, your father and I too were deeply anguished, *and* were searching for you!"[l]

42 And he said to them, "Why were you searching for me? Did you not know that I should be among the *children* of my Father?"[m]

43 And they did not understand the statement that he spoke to them.[n]

44 And he went down with them and he came to Nazareth, and he was subject to them.[o]

45 And Jesus advanced in wisdom[p] and stature and [6]favor with God and men.[q]

---

6 Or, *grace*

John the Baptist

Chapter 2

Now in those days, John came baptising in the wilderness,[a] preaching a baptism of repentance for the forgiveness of sins,[b]

2 and saying, "Repent, for the kingdom of the heavens has drawn near."[c]

3 For this is the *one who was* spoken of through Isaiah the prophet, saying,

> "A VOICE OF ONE CRYING IN THE WILDERNESS,
> 'PREPARE THE WAY OF THE LORD,
> MAKE HIS PATHS STRAIGHT.'"[d]

4 Moreover, John was clothed in camel's hair, and about his waist *he wore* a leather belt, and he was eating locusts and wild honey.[e]

5 At that time, Jerusalem went out to him, and all Judea, and all the neighboring *areas* of Jordan,[f]

6 and were baptised by him in the Jordan River, confessing their sins.[g]

---

a Isa 40:3
   Mal 3:1
   Mt 3:1
b Mr 1:4
   Lu 3:3
c Isa 65:17
   Da 2:44
   Da 4:3
   Da 6:26
   Da 7:14,27
   Mt 3:2
d Ps 68:4
   Isa 35:8-10
   Isa 40:3
   Isa 57:14
   Isa 62:10
   Mt 3:3
   Mr 1:2
   Jn 1:23
e Mt 3:4
   Mr 1:6
f Mt 3:5
   Mr 1:5
g Nu 5:6,7
   Mt 3:6
   Mr 1:5

7 But having seen the many Pharisees and Sadducees coming to his baptism, he said to them, "Children of vipers, who warned you to flee from the coming wrath?[h]

8 "Produce therefore fruit worthy of repentance, and do not think to say within yourselves, '*For* father we have Abraham';[i] for I say to you, that God is able to raise up children to Abraham from these stones.[j]

9 "But the axe is already laid at the root of the trees. Therefore, every tree not bearing beautiful fruit is cut down with the axe and thrown into *the* fire."[k]

10 And the multitudes questioned him, saying, "What then shall we do?"[l]

11 And answering, he was saying to them, "He that has two tunics, let him share with him that has none; and he that has food, let him do likewise."[m]

12 And *some* tax collectors also came to him to be baptised, and they said to him, "Teacher, what shall we do?"[n]

13 And he said to them, "Collect nothing more than what you have been ordered to."[o]

14 And *some* soldiers were also questioning him, saying, "And what shall we do?" And he said to them,

The preaching of John the Baptist

"Coerce no one, nor accuse *anyone* falsely;[p] and be content with your wages."[q]

15 Now the people were waiting for and were all reasoning in their hearts about John, *as to* whether or not he might be the [1]messiah.[r]

16 John answered, saying to *them* all, "Indeed, I baptise you *with* water, but He who is mightier than I is coming,[s] of whom I am not worthy to untie the thong of His sandals[t] – He will baptise you with holy spirit and fire;[u]

17 whose winnowing fork is in His hand[v] – He will thoroughly cleanse His threshing floor, and will gather the wheat into His barn, but He will burn up the chaff with an unquenchable fire.[w]

18 "'FOR THEY ARE A PERVERSE GENERATION, SONS IN WHOM THERE IS NO FAITHFULNESS.[x]

19 "'IN MY ANGER,[y] I HAVE IGNITED A FIRE,[z] AND IT WILL BURN DOWN TO THE DEPTHS OF SHEOL;[a]

20 MY ANGER WILL BLAZE AGAINST THEM, AND I WILL ANNIHILATE THEM.[b]

21 "'FOR VENGEANCE IS MINE,' SAYS THE LORD. 'THE DAY OF THEIR DISASTER IS NEAR, AND THE

s Ps 96:13
   Ps 98:9
   Zec 2:10
t Ps 60:8
   Ps 108:9
   Jn 1:27
u Isa 4:4
   Isa 33:10-14
   Isa 63:10
   Mt 3:11
   Mr 1:8
   Lu 3:16
v Mic 4:12
w De 4:24
   Pr 29:19
   Isa 5:24,25
   Na 1:6
   Mal 4:1
   Mt 3:12
   Lu 3:17
x De 32:20
   Pr 29:21
   Isa 1:2
   Isa 30:9
   Isa 44:21
y Ex 34:14
   Pr 6:34
   Pr 29:11
   Ec 7:9
   Jer 25:30-38
z De 4:24
   Ps 79:5
   Pr 27:4
   Ca 8:6
   Isa 30:27,30
   Jer 15:14
   Eze 22:20-22
a De 32:22
b Nu 11:1,3
   De 6:15
   De 7:4
   Isa 5:25
   Isa 29:6
   Isa 66:16
   Jer 23:29
   Eze 21:31,32
   Eze 22:31
   Na 1:2,6
   Mal 4:1

---

1 Gr., *messias*, for the Hebrew *mashiach*; certain later mss. read, *christos*

Jesus is baptised by John the Baptist

EVENTS THAT AWAIT THEM ARE SOON TO COME.[c]

22 "'FOR THE LORD WILL JUDGE HIS PEOPLE.'"[d]

23 And it happened in those days, that Jesus came from Nazareth in Galilee, and was baptised in the Jordan by John.[e]

24 And again, on the following day, John was standing, and two of his disciples;[f]

25 and having looked on Jesus walking, he said, "Behold, the lamb of God."[g]

26 And the two disciples heard him speaking, and they followed Jesus.[h]

27 But having turned, and having seen them following *him*, he said to them, "What are you seeking?" And they said to him, "Rabbi, where are you staying?"[i]

28 And he said to them, "Come and see." So they went and saw where he was staying, and they stayed with him that day, about the ²tenth hour.[j]

29 And Andrew, the brother of Simon, was one of the two having heard this from John, and having followed him.[k]

30 He found his own brother Simon first, and —

---
2 I.e., 4 p.m.

---

c De 32:35
Isa 13:6,9
Joe 1:15
Joe 2:1,11
d Ps 50:4
Eze 5:8
Eze 7:3
Eze 20:36,37
Eze 33:20
Mt 7:1,2
e Mt 3:13
Mr 1:9
Lu 3:21
f Jn 1:35
g Ge 22:8,13
Isa 53:7,10
Jn 1:36
h Jn 1:37
i Jn 1:38
j Jn 1:39
k Jn 1:40

saying to him, "We have found the ³messiah" — he led him to Jesus.ˡ

31 On the following day, he was wanting to go forth into Galilee, and finding Philip, Jesus said to him, "Follow me!"ᵐ

32 Now Philip was from Bethsaida, the city of Andrew and Simon.ⁿ

33 Philip found Nathanael, and said to him, "We have found *him* of whom Moses wrote in the law, and the prophets, Jesus of Nazareth."⁴ ᵒ

34 And Nathanael said to him, "Can any good thing come out of Nazareth?" Philip said to him, "Come and see."ᵖ

35 Jesus saw Nathanael coming to him, and he said about him, "Behold, truly an Israelite, in whom *there* is no ⁵deceit."ᑫ

36 Nathanael said to him, "From where do you know me?" Jesus answered and said to him, "Before Philip called *you*, being under the fig tree, I saw you."ʳ

37 Nathanael answered him, "Rabbi, you are the son of God, you are the king of Israel."ˢ

l Jn 1:41,42
m Jn 1:43
n Jn 1:44
o De 18:15
   Isa 11:1
   Zec 3:8
   Jn 1:45
p Jn 1:46
q Ge 27:30-35,40
   Jn 1:47
r 1Ki 4:25
   Mic 4:4
   Zec 3:10
   Jn 1:48
s De 17:15
   Ps 2:6-9
   Jer 23:5
   Jn 1:49

---

3 Gr., *messian*, for the Hebrew *mashiach*
4 Certain later mss. add, *the son of Joseph*
5 Or, *guile*

Jesus is tempted by Satan in the wilderness

t Ex 13:21
   Ne 9:19-21
   Ps 78:14
   Lu 4:1
u Ex 24:15,18
   De 2:7
v Ge 22:1
   Ex 20:20
   De 8:2
   Ps 26:2
w Mt 4:1
   Mr 1:13
   Lu 4:2
   Jn 20:12
x Ex 34:28
   De 9:9
y Ps 107:5
   Mt 4:2
   Lu 4:2
z Jn 8:44
a Ex 4:22
   De 14:1,2
b Ex 24:12
   De 9:11
c Ps 78:18
   Mt 4:3
   Mt 7:9
   Lu 4:3
d Ex 20:1-17
   Le 18:5
   De 4:1,2
   De 8:3
   De 32:45-47
   Jer 15:16
   Mt 4:4
   Lu 4:4
e Ps 82:6
f Mt 4:5,6
   Lu 4:9
g Ps 91:11
   Mt 4:6
   Lu 4:10
h Ps 91:12
   Mt 4:6
   Lu 4:11
i De 6:16
   Mt 4:7
   Lu 4:12
j Nu 27:12
   De 32:49

38 But Jesus, full of holy spirit, returned from the Jordan, and was led by the spirit into the wilderness.^{t}

39 And he was in the wilderness for forty days,^{u} being ^{6}tempted by Satan;^{v} and he was with the wild beasts, and the angels were serving him.^{w}

40 And having fasted forty days and forty nights,^{x} afterwards he was hungry.^{y}

41 Then the tempter,^{z} having come near, said to him, "If you are *a* son of the god,^{a} ^{7}ask, that these stones^b might become loaves of bread."^{c}

42 But answering, he said, "It has been written, IT IS NOT BY BREAD THAT MAN DOES LIVE, BUT BY EVERY WORD THAT PROCEEDS FROM THE MOUTH OF GOD."^{d}

43 Then the devil led him to Jerusalem, and stood him upon the temple's ^{8}pinnacle, and said to him, "If you are *a* son of the god,^{e} *then* cast yourself down from here,^{f}

44 for it has been written, HE WILL COMMAND HIS ANGELS CONCERNING YOU,^{g}

45 and IN THEIR HANDS THEY WILL RAISE YOU

---

6 Or, *tested*
7 According to the best ancient mss.; most later mss. read, *speak*
8 Or, *battlement*

Satan departs

UP, LEST EVER YOU SHOULD STRIKE YOUR FOOT AGAINST A STONE."ʰ

46 And answering, Jesus said to him, "Again, it is written, YOU SHALL NOT TEST THE LORD YOUR GOD."ⁱ

47 And the devil, having led him up to a high mountain,ʲ showed him all the kingdoms of the inhabited world, in a moment of time;ᵏ

48 and the devil said to him, "I will give to you all this domain,ˡ and their glory, for it has been handed over to me,ᵐ and I give it to whomever I wish.ⁿ

49 "If you will therefore fear and serve me,ᵒ and swear by my name,ᵖ then I will give this all to you,ᑫ and EVERY PLACE ON WHICH THE SOLES OF YOUR FEET SHALL TREAD SHALL BE YOURS."ʳ

50 And answering, Jesus said to him, "Depart, Satan! How shall it benefit a man if he gains the whole world, yet loses himself;ˢ for what shall a man give in exchange for his soul,ᵗ once he has lost it ⁹forever?"ᵘ

51 And having finished every temptation, the devil departed from him, until *an* opportune time.ᵛ

---
9 Lit., *to the age*

k Ge 13:14,15
   De 34:1-4
   Mt 4:8
   Lu 4:5
l Ge 13:14,15
   Ge 26:3,4
   Ge 28:13,14
m Ex 19:5
   De 10:14
   Ps 24:1
   Ps 89:11
   Nu 14:8
n Jer 27:5
   Da 4:17
   Lu 4:6
o De 5:29
   De 6:24
   De 10:12
   De 13:4
   De 28:58-63
   Ps 34:9,11
p De 6:13
   De 10:20
q Ge 17:7,8
   Ps 2:8
   Ps 37:22
   Isa 1:19
   Mt 4:9
   Lu 4:7
r De 11:22-24
   Jos 1:3
s Le 25:55
   Isa 44:21
   Mr 8:36
   Lu 9:25
t De 10:12
   Ps 49:8
   Eze 18:4
   Mt 16:26
   Mr 8:37
u Ge 17:7
   Job 41:4
   Ps 105:8
   Isa 44:21
   Jer 5:23
   Jer 31:31-33
   Jer 32:38-40
   Eze 11:19,20
   Eze 36:26,27
v Na 1:9
   Lu 4:13

Chapter 3

N<small>OW</small> having heard that John had been handed over,[a] he withdrew into Galilee.[b]

2   And having left Nazareth, *and* having come, he settled in Capernaum,[c] which is by the sea.[d]

3   And as he was passing by the sea of Galilee, he saw Simon, and Andrew, the brother of Simon, casting a net into the sea; for they were fishermen.[e]

4   And he said to them, "Come, follow me!"[f] And immediately, they left their nets and followed him.[g]

5   And having gone on from there, he saw others, two brothers, James the *son* of Zebedee, and John, his brother, in the boat with Zebedee, their father, preparing their nets.[h]

6   And at that moment he called them; and having left their father Zebedee in the boat with the hired servants, they went away after him.[i]

7   And when he came to Capernaum, immediately

---

[a] Mt 14:3
    Mr 6:17
    Lu 3:20
[b] Mt 4:12
    Mr 1:14
    Lu 4:14
[c] Mr 2:1
[d] Mt 4:13
[e] Mt 4:18
    Mr 1:16
[f] Mt 4:19
    Mr 1:17
[g] Mt 4:20
    Mr 1:18
[h] Mt 4:21
    Mr 1:19
[i] Mt 4:21,22
    Mr 1:20

Jesus teaches in Capernaum

on the Sabbath, Jesus entered the synagogue and was teaching.[j]

8 And they were thunderstruck by his teaching, for he was teaching them as *one* having authority, and not as the scribes.[k]

9 [1][And at that moment in their synagogue there was a man with *an* unclean spirit, and he cried out,[l]

10 saying, "What do these people have to do with you, Jesus of Nazareth? Have you come to destroy us?[m] I know who you are – the holy *one* of God!"[n]

11 And Jesus rebuked him, saying, "Be quiet, and come forth out of him!"[o]

12 And the unclean spirit, having convulsed him, and having shouted with a great voice, came out of him.[p]]

13 And all were astonished, so as to question among themselves, saying, "What is this new teaching, with *such* authority? [1][He commands even the unclean spirits, and they obey him!"[q]]

14 And the news about him went out immediately into all the surrounding area of Galilee.[r]

15 And having left the synagogue, immediately

---

[j] Mr 1:21; Lu 4:31
[k] Mt 7:28,29; Mr 1:22; Lu 4:32
[l] Mr 1:23; Lu 4:33
[m] De 13:1,3
[n] Mr 1:24; Lu 4:34
[o] Mr 1:25; Lu 4:35
[p] Mr 1:26; Lu 4:35
[q] Mr 1:27; Lu 4:36
[r] Mr 1:28; Lu 4:37

---

1 Verses 9-12 and part of verse 13 are not found in the best ancient mss.

Jesus departs to a solitary place

they came into the house of Simon and Andrew, with James and John,[s]

16 for Simon's mother-in-law was lying ill with fever; and immediately they spoke to him about her.[t]

17 And having come to *her*, he raised her up, having taken her hand; and the fever left her, and she served them.[u]

18 But at the setting of the sun, all those who were ill with various sicknesses were brought to him, and having laid the hands on each one of them, he healed them.[v]

19 And in the very early morning, when it was still night, he arose and went out and departed *by himself* to a solitary place to pray.[w]

20 And Simon and those with him went searching for him;[x] and having found him, they reproached him, saying, "Everyone is looking for you!"[y]

21 But he said to them, "Let us go *by* another way, into the neighboring towns, that I might preach also there. It was for this that I left *the house*."[z]

22 And he was preaching in the synagogues of Galilee.[a]

23 And having returned again to Capernaum after

---

[s] Mt 8:14; Mr 1:29; Lu 4:38
[t] Mt 8:14; Mr 1:30; Lu 4:38
[u] Mt 8:15; Mr 1:31; Lu 4:39
[v] Mr 1:32,34; Lu 4:40
[w] Ps 19:2; Ps 119:15,147; Ps 143:5; Mr 1:35; Lu 4:42; Lu 5:16
[x] Mr 1:36; Lu 4:42
[y] Mr 1:37
[z] Mr 1:38; Lu 4:43
[a] Mt 4:23; Mr 1:39; Lu 4:44

The paralytic   Levi is called

some days, and it was heard that he was in a house.[b]

24 And behold, they brought to him a paralytic, lying on a mat; and seeing their faith, Jesus said to the paralytic, "Take heart, child – your sins have been forgiven."[c]

25 But some of the scribes said within themselves, "He blasphemes."[d]

26 But Jesus, having perceived their thoughts, said to them, "Why do you think evil in your hearts?[e]

27 "For which is easier – to say, 'Your sins have been forgiven you', or to say, 'Rise up and walk'?[f]

28 "But that you might know that the son of man on the earth has authority to forgive sins –" he said to the paralytic, "Take up your mat and go away to your house."[g]

29 And having gotten up, he went away to his house.[h]

30 And he went out again by the sea, and all the crowd came to him, and he taught them.[i]

31 And passing by, he saw Levi, the *son* of Alphaeus, sitting in the tax collector's booth, and he said, "Follow me!" And he rose and followed him.[j]

32 And it came about, that as he was reclining in

b Mr 2:1
c Ex 34:7
   Nu 14:18
   Jer 32:18
   Mt 9:2
   Mr 2:5
   Lu 5:20
d Mt 9:3
   Mr 2:6,7
   Lu 5:21
e Mt 9:4
   Mr 2:8
   Lu 5:22
f Mt 9:5
   Mr 2:9
   Lu 5:23
g Mt 9:6
   Mr 2:10,11
   Lu 5:24
h Mt 9:7
i Mr 2:13
j Mt 9:9
   Mr 2:14
   Lu 5:27,28

3 The scribes of the Pharisees question Jesus   Fasting

k Ec 5:18
Ec 8:15
Ec 9:7
Mt 9:10
Mt 11:19
Lu 7:34
l Mr 2:15
Lu 15:1
m Isa 22:13
Jer 16:8
Mt 9:11
Mr 2:16
Lu 5:30
Lu 15:2
n De 28:58-61
Isa 1:5,6
Jer 15:18
Jer 30:12-15
Mt 9:12
Mr 2:17
Lu 5:31
o 1Ki 8:46
Job 25:4-6
Ps 143:2
Pr 20:9
Ec 7:20
p Mt 9:13
Mr 2:17
Lu 5:32
q Joe 2:12
Lu 18:11,12
r Mt 9:14
Mr 2:18
Lu 5:33
Lu 18:11,12
s Isa 22:12
t Isa 22:13
Mt 9:15
Mr 2:19
Lu 5:34

the house, many tax collectors and sinners came, and they were reclining at table with Jesus and his disciples;[k] for there were many of them, and they were following him.[l]

33 And the scribes of the Pharisees, having seen him eating with the sinners and tax collectors, said to his disciples, "Why does he eat with tax collectors and sinners?"[m]

34 And hearing this, Jesus said to them, "It is not those who are healthy who need a physician, but those who are sick.[n]

35 "But rather, go and learn what *this* means, 'NO MAN IS RIGHTEOUS AND DOES NOT SIN.'[o] I did not come to call the righteous, but sinners."[p]

36 And John's disciples and the Pharisees were fasting; and they came to him, saying, "Why do John's disciples and the Pharisees' disciples fast,[q] yet you and your disciples do not fast?"[r]

37 And Jesus said to them, "Can the sons of the bridal chamber fast,[s] while the bridegroom is *there* with them? As long as they have the bridegroom with them, they cannot fast.[t]

38 "But the days will come when the bridegroom

will have been taken away from them,[u] and then will they fast.[v]

39 "No one sews a piece of new cloth on an old garment, lest the patch pulls away from it, the new from the old, and a worse tear occurs.[w]

40 "And no one puts new wine into old wineskins,[x] lest the wine burst the wineskins, and the wine and the wineskins are utterly destroyed; but new wine *is put* into fresh wineskins, and both are preserved.[y]

41 "Yet no one who has drunk the old desires new, for he says the old *wine* is good."[z]

42 And it came about that he was passing through the grain fields on the Sabbath, and his disciples began to make their way, picking the heads of grain.[a]

43 But some of the Pharisees said, "Why are you doing what is not lawful on the Sabbath?"[b]

44 And he said to them, "Have you not read what David did when he was in need and was hungry, he and those who were with him;[c]

45 how he entered into the house of God in *the time of* Abiathar, *who became* high priest,[d] and *he* ate the consecrated bread,[e] which is not lawful *for anyone* to eat, except for the priests,[f] and he even gave *it* to those

u Isa 22:14
   Isa 53:8
v Mt 9:15
   Mr 2:20
   Lu 5:35
w Mt 9:16
   Mr 2:21
   Lu 5:36
x Jer 51:26
y Mt 9:17
   Mr 2:22
   Lu 5:37,38
z Isa 25:6
   Lu 5:39
a De 23:25
   Mt 12:1
   Mr 2:23
   Lu 6:1
b Ex 20:8-11
   Ex 31:13-17
   Mt 12:2
   Mr 2:24
   Lu 6:2
c Mt 12:3
   Mr 2:25
   Lu 6:3
d 1Sa 21:1
e Ex 25:30
f Le 24:5-9

3   The Sabbath

who were with him?[g]

46 "Or, have you not read in the Law that the priests in the temple[h] break the Sabbath,[i] and *yet* are guiltless?"[j]

47 And he said to them, "The Sabbath was made for the sake of man,[k] and not man for the sake of the Sabbath. Therefore, the son of man is master also of the Sabbath."[l]

48 And it came to pass on another Sabbath, that he entered into the synagogue and was teaching, and there was a man there, whose right hand was withered.[m]

49 And he said to them, "Is it lawful on the Sabbath to do good, or to do evil? To save a life, or to kill?" But they were silent.[n]

50 And having looked around on them with seething anger, being grieved by the hardness of their heart, he said to the man, "Stretch out your hand." And having taken hold *of him*, he laid on the hands, and he healed him, and let *him* go.[o]

51 And he said to them, "Which one of you shall have a donkey or an ox fall into a pit, and will not immediately pull him out on the Sabbath day?[p]

52 "Then how much more valuable is a man than

---

g 1Sa 21:3-6
   Mt 12:4
   Mr 2:26
   Lu 6:4
h Le 1:7
   Le 6:12,13
   Nu 28:2,9,10
i   Ex 31:14,15
   Ex 35:2,3
j   Mt 12:5
k Ex 23:12
   De 5:14
l   Mt 12:8
   Mr 2:27,28
   Lu 6:5
m Mt 12:9,10
   Mr 3:1
   Lu 6:6
n Mr 3:4
   Lu 12:57
   Lu 14:3,4
o Mt 12:13
   Mr 3:5
   Lu 14:4
p Mt 12:11
   Lu 14:5

a sheep! Therefore, it is lawful to do good on the Sabbath."ᑫ

53 And they were not able to reply to these *things*.ʳ

q *Mt 12:12*
r *Lu 14:6*

Chapter 4

Now it came to pass in these days, that he went out to the mountain to pray, and he was spending the whole night in prayer to God.ᵃ

2 And when it became day, he called to *him* those he wanted, and they went to him.ᵇ

3 And he appointed twelve, that they might be with him, and that he might send them out to preach.ᶜ

4 And to Simon he was applying the name Cephas;ᵈ

5 and James, the *son* of Zebedee, and John, the brother of James,ᵉ and he was applying to them the name ¹Boanerges;ᶠ

a *Lu 5:16*
  Lu 6:12
  Lu 11:9
b *Mr 3:13*
  Lu 6:13
c *Mr 3:14*
d *Mt 10:2*
  Mr 3:16
  Lu 6:14
e *Mt 10:2*
  Lu 6:14
f *Mr 3:17*

---

1 Of Aramaic origin; possibly, *sons of thunder*

The Gospel of Jesus of Nazareth

The Beatitudes

<small>
g Mt 10:2,3
  Mr 3:18
  Lu 6:14,15
h Mt 10:4
  Mt 19:30
  Mt 20:16
  Mr 3:18,19
  Lu 6:15,16
i Mr 3:7
  Lu 6:17
j De 28:58-60
k Lu 6:18
l Lu 6:19
m Mr 3:9
n Mt 5:2
o La 1:7
p Mt 5:3
  Lu 6:20
</small>

6 and Andrew; and Philip; and Bartholomew; and Matthew; and Thomas; and James, the *son* of Alphaeus; and Thaddaeus;[g]

7 and Simon, the Zealous; and [2]Judas, the [3]Iscariot.[h]

8 And having descended with them, he stood on a level place; and *there was* a large crowd of his disciples, and a great multitude of people from Galilee,[4][i]

9 who came to hear him and to be healed of their sicknesses;[j] and those *who were* troubled by unclean spirits were cared for.[k]

10 And all the crowd sought to touch him, for power went out from him and healed all.[l]

11 And he spoke to his disciples, that a boat might stand ready for him, on account of the crowd, that they might not press upon him.[m]

12 And having opened his mouth, he taught them, saying,[n]

13 "Blessed *are* the poor,[o] for yours is the kingdom of God.[p]

<small>
2 Gr., *Ioudas*, for the Hebrew *Yehudah*
3 Meaning uncertain; certain later mss. add, *who also handed him over*
4 Certain later mss. add, *and from all Judea and Jerusalem, and the sea coast of Tyre and Sidon*
</small>

Love your enemies 4

14 "Blessed *are* those who are hungering[q] now, for you will be filled.[r]

15 "Blessed *are* those *who are* weeping[s] now, for you will laugh.[t]

16 "You have heard that it was said, YOU SHALL LOVE YOUR NEIGHBOR[u] and HATE YOUR ENEMY.[v]

17 "But I say to you who hear, love your enemies,[w] *and* do well to those who hate you.[x]

18 "You have heard that it was said, AN EYE FOR AN EYE, AND A TOOTH FOR A TOOTH.[y]

19 "But I say to you, to him who strikes you on the cheek, offer *him* also the other; and from him who takes away your cloak, do not withhold the tunic.[z]

20 "To every one *who* asks you, give; and from him who takes away what *is* yours, do not ask *for it* back.[a]

21 "And just as you desire that men should do to you, do to them in the same way.[b]

22 "And if you love *only* those who love you, what credit is that to you?[c] For even sinners love those who love them.[d]

23 "And if you do good *only* to those who do good to you, what credit is that to you?[e] For even sinners do likewise.[f]

[q] La 2:12,20
La 3:1,43
La 4:4,9
[r] Mt 5:6
Lu 6:21
[s] La 1:12
La 2:5,11
La 3:48,49
La 5:7,8
[t] Lu 6:21
[u] Le 19:17,18
Le 19:33,34
[v] De 7:2,16,24
De 20:17
Ps 18:37,38,40
Ps 139:22
Mt 5:43
[w] Ex 23:22,23,27
[x] De 5:9
De 7:10
De 32:41
Mt 5:44
Lu 6:27
[y] Ex 21:24,25
Le 24:17-21
De 19:21
Mt 5:38
[z] Mt 5:39,40
Lu 6:29
[a] Mt 5:42
Lu 6:30
[b] Mt 7:12
Lu 6:31
[c] Ex 20:5,6
De 7:9
Ps 103:11
[d] Mt 5:46
Lu 6:32
[e] Nu 14:8
De 30:9,10
Ps 18:25
Isa 1:19
Jer 7:23
[f] Lu 6:33

The Gospel of Jesus of Nazareth

24 "And if you lend *to those* from whom you expect to receive, what credit is that to you?[g] For even sinners lend to sinners, so that they might receive back the same.[h]

25 "But love your enemies, and do good,[i] and lend, expecting nothing in return;[j]

26 and be [5]compassionate, just as your Father is [6]compassionate[k] – for He makes His sun rise on *both* evil and good, and sends rain on *both the* righteous and unrighteous.[l]

27 "Judge not, that you not be judged;[m] and do not condemn,[n] that you not be condemned.[o] [6]Release,[p] and you will be [7]released.[q]

28 "For with the judgment that you judge,[r] you will be judged;[s] and with the measure that you measure,[t] it will be measured to you.[u]

29 "But why do you see the speck in your brother's eye,[v] and do not perceive the beam *that is* in your own eye?[w]

30 "How can you say to your brother, 'Let me take out the speck that *is* in your eye', when you yourself do

---

5 Or, *merciful*
6 Or, *set free; send away*
7 Or, *set free; sent away*

Each tree is known by its fruit

not see the beam in your own eye?[x]

31 "Hypocrite! First pull out the beam from your own eye, and then you will see clearly the speck that is in your brother's eye.[y]

32 "For there is no good tree, producing bad fruit;[z] nor again a bad tree, producing good fruit.[a]

33 "For each tree is known by its own fruit.[b] For they do not gather figs from thorn bushes, nor do they gather a cluster of grapes from a bramble.[c]

34 "The good man, out of the good treasure of the heart, brings forth that which *is* good; and the bad *one*, out of the bad *treasure*, brings forth that which *is* bad. For his mouth speaks from that which fills his heart.[d]

35 "Again, you have heard that it was said to the ancients, YOU SHALL NOT SWEAR FALSELY,[e] BUT YOU SHALL KEEP YOUR VOWS TO THE LORD,[f] and YOU SHALL SWEAR BY HIS NAME.[g]

36 "But I say to you, do not swear at all — neither by the sky, because it is the throne of God,[h]

37 nor by the earth,[i] because it is a footstool for His feet;[j] nor by Jerusalem, because it is the city of the great King.[k]

---

w De 4:31
   Ps 94:14
   Isa 49:15
   Jer 12:7
   Jer 23:39,40
   La 5:20,22
   Mt 7:3
   Mt 27:46
   Mr 15:34
   Lu 6:41
x Mt 7:4
   Lu 6:42
y Mt 7:5
   Lu 6:42
z Ge 1:12
   Ge 2:8,9
   Ge 3:6,22
a Mt 7:18
   Lu 6:43
b Ex 3:13,14
   Ex 4:22
   De 14:1
   Ps 78:36,37
   Isa 1:2
   Isa 30:9
   Isa 63:10
   Isa 64:8
c Mt 7:16
   Lu 6:44
d De 28:15-68
   Jer 9:11
   Eze 7:2-9
   Eze 7:25-27
   Eze 21:3-5
   Eze 22:19-22
   Mt 12:34,35
   Lu 6:45
e Le 19:12
f Nu 30:2
   De 23:21,23
   Ps 66:13
   Ps 76:11
   Mt 5:33
g De 6:13
   De 10:20
h Isa 66:1
   Mt 5:34
i Isa 65:16
j Isa 66:1
k Ps 48:2
   Mt 5:35

His own people come for him

l Mt 5:36
m Mt 5:37
n Le 2:1-3
   Le 2:9,13
o Le 2:13
   Mr 9:49
p Job 6:6,7
q Mr 9:50
r Mt 5:13
s Mr 9:50
t Lu 7:1
u Mr 3:20

38 "Nor shall you swear by your own head, for you cannot turn one hair white or black.^{l}

39 "But your word 'yes' *must* be 'yes', *and* 'no', 'no'; anything more *than* this comes from the bad treasure.^{m}

40 "You have heard that it was said, EVERY GRAIN OFFERING BY FIRE SHALL BE SALTED,^{n} and EVERY SACRIFICE SHALL BE SALTED WITH SALT.^{o}

41 "Therefore, salt is good. But if the salt becomes tasteless,^{p} with what will you season it?^{q} It is fit for nothing, except, having been cast out, to be trampled underfoot by men.^{r}

42 "Have salt in yourselves, and be at peace with one another."^{s}

43 And when he had fulfilled saying all of his words in the hearing of the people, he entered into Capernaum.^{t}

44 And he came into a house, and again a crowd gathered, so that they were not able to eat even bread.^{u}

45 And ^{8}his own people, having heard *of this*, went out to seize him; for they were saying, "He is out of

---
8 Lit., *those of him*

"Behold, my mother and my brothers" — 4

his mind,^v because he has an unclean spirit."^w

46 And his mother and his brothers arrived, and they were standing outside;^x and they sent *word* to him, calling him.^y

47 And a crowd was sitting around him, and they said to him, "Behold, your mother and your brothers^z are outside, and are asking for you."^a

48 And answering them, he said, "Who is my mother, and *who are* my brothers?"^b

49 And having looked about on those who were sitting around him in a circle, he said, "Behold, my mother^c and my brothers."^d

50 But answering, he said to them, "My mother and my brothers are those who are hearing and doing the word of God."^e

51 And a certain woman from the crowd, having raised *her* voice, said to him, "Blessed *is* the womb that bore you, and *the* breasts at which you nursed!"^f

52 But he said, "On the contrary, blessed are they who hear the word,^g and keep watch *over it*."^h

v Ho 9:7
  Na 1:11
w Ps 69:9
  Mr 3:21,30
x Mt 12:46
  Lu 8:19
  Jn 7:5
y Mr 3:31
z Ps 69:8
  Mt 13:55
a Mt 12:47
  Mr 3:32
  Lu 8:20
b Ps 69:8
  Mt 12:48
  Mr 3:33
c Jn 19:25
d Ps 113:9
  Mt 12:49
  Mr 3:34
e Mt 12:50
  Mr 3:35
  Lu 8:21
f Lu 11:27
g Mr 4:14
h Lu 11:28

Chapter 5

^a *Lu 8:1*
^b *Lu 8:2*
^c *Lu 8:3*
^d *Mt 13:1,2*
  Mr 4:1
^e *Mt 13:3*
  Mr 4:2
^f *Mt 13:3*
  Mr 4:3
  Lu 8:5

AND it came about, soon afterwards, that he journeyed through city and village, proclaiming and announcing the good news of the kingdom of God; and the twelve *were* with him,^a

2   and certain women *as well*, who had been healed from evil spirits and weaknesses – Mary who is called Magdalene, from whom seven demons had gone out,^b

3   and Joanna, *the* wife of Chuza, Herod's steward, and Susanna, and many others – who were serving them out of their own means.^c

4   And again, he began to teach by the sea. And the crowd that was gathered together became so great, that he got into a boat on the sea and sat down; and all the crowd was on the shore, close to the sea.^d

5   And he was teaching them many things in parables, and saying to them in his teaching,^e

6   "Listen! Behold, the sower went out to sow.^f

The parable of the sower

7 "And it came to pass, as he sowed, that some *seed* fell beside the road, and the birds came and devoured it.^g

8 "And other *seed* fell on the rocky *ground*, and where it had not much soil; and immediately it sprang up, because it had no depth of soil.^h

9 "And after the sun rose, it was scorched; and because it had no root, it withered.ⁱ

10 "And other *seed* fell among the thorns, and the thorns grew up, and choked it, and it gave no fruit.^j

11 "And other *seed* fell into the good soil, and gave fruit, growing up and increasing, and bore in one thirty, and in one sixty, and in one a hundred."^k

12 And he was saying, "He who has ears to hear,^l let him hear."^m

13 And when he was alone, those about him, with the twelve, asked him *about* the parable.ⁿ

14 And he said to them, "You do not understand this parable? And how will you understand all the parables?^o

15 "The sower sows the word.^p

16 "And these are the ones who are beside the road^q where the word is sown: and when they hear *it*,

g Mt 13:4
  Mr 4:4
  Lu 8:5
h Mt 13:5
  Mr 4:5
  Lu 8:6
i Mt 13:6
  Mr 4:6
  Lu 8:6
j Mt 13:7
  Mr 4:7
  Lu 8:7
k Mt 13:8
  Mr 4:8
  Lu 8:8
l De 29:4
  Isa 6:9,10
m Pr 2:2,10
  Mt 13:9
  Mr 4:9
  Lu 8:8
n Mt 13:10
  Mr 4:10
  Lu 8:9
o Mr 4:13
p De 4:2
  De 13:1-5
  Mr 4:14
q Isa 35:8
  Jer 6:16
  Jer 18:15

The Gospel of Jesus of Nazareth

5   Jesus explains the parable of the sower

immediately Satan comes and takes away the word[r] that has been sown in them.[s]

17 "And likewise, these are the ones who upon the rocky *ground* are sown: who, when they hear the word, immediately receive it with joy;[t]

18 and they have no root in themselves, but are temporary — then affliction or persecution having arisen[u] on account of the word immediately causes them to stumble.[v]

19 "And these are the ones who among the thorns are sown: these are the *ones*, having heard the word;[w]

20 and the worries of the age, and the illusion of riches, and desires for the rest enter in,[x] choking the word, and it becomes unfruitful.[y]

21 "And these are the ones who upon the good ground have been sown: those who hear the word and receive it, and bring forth fruit, in one thirty, and in one sixty, and in one a hundred."[z]

22 And he was saying to them, "Is a lamp brought to be put under the basket, or under the bed? *Is it* not *brought* that it might be put upon the lampstand?[a]

23 "For nothing is hidden,[b] except that it should be brought to light;[c] nor has *anything* secret[d] come into

The kingdom of God

being, but that it should come to light.[e]

24 "Therefore, look at how you hear. For whoever might have, *more* will be given to him, and whoever might not have, even what he seems to have will be taken *away* from him."[f]

25 And he was saying, "The kingdom of God is in this way like a man who should cast the seed upon the earth,[g]

26 and should sleep and rise night and day; and the seed should sprout and grow — he knows not how.[h]

27 "The earth itself brings forth fruit — first a blade, then a head of grain, then full grain in the head.[i]

28 "But when the fruit should be handed over, immediately he sends the sickle, for the harvest stands ready.[j]

29 "Therefore, to what shall we liken the kingdom of God, or with what parable shall we describe it?[k]

30 "It is like a mustard seed, which is the smallest of all the seeds upon the earth,[l]

31 yet when it is full grown, it is larger than all the garden plants, and forms large branches, and the birds of the sky find shelter in its shade."[m]

32 And again he was saying, "To what will I liken

---

e Mt 10:26
  Mr 4:22
  Lu 12:2
  Jn 3:20
  Jn 8:32
f Mr 4:25
  Lu 8:18
g Mr 4:26
h Ec 7:24
  Ec 8:17
  Ec 11:5
i Mr 4:27
j Mr 4:28
k Isa 40:18
  Mr 4:30
  Lu 13:18
l Mt 13:31
  Mr 4:31
  Lu 13:19
m Mt 13:32
  Mr 4:32
  Lu 13:19

Jesus gives orders to depart

the kingdom of God?[n]

33 "It is like leaven, which a woman took and hid in three ¹measures of flour, until it was all leavened."[o]

34 And with many such parables was he speaking the word to them, as they were able to hear *it*;[p]

35 nor was he speaking to them without parables;[q] *yet* he was explaining everything in private to his own disciples.[r]

36 And on that day, when evening had come, he said to them, "Let us go over to the other side."[s]

37 ²[And having come up to him, one scribe said to him, "Teacher, I will follow you wherever you might go."[t]

38 And Jesus said to him, "Foxes have holes, and the birds of the air have nests, but the son of man has not where he might rest *his* head."[u]

39 But another of his disciples said to him, "Master, allow me to first go and bury my father."[v]

40 But Jesus said to him, "Follow me, and leave the dead to bury the dead themselves."[w]]

41 And sending away the crowd, they took him

---

n *Mt 13:33*
  Lu 13:20
o *Mt 13:33*
  Lu 13:21
p *Mr 4:33*
q *Mt 13:34*
r *Mr 4:34*
s *Mt 8:18*
  Mr 4:35
  Lu 8:22
t *Mt 8:19*
  Lu 9:57
u *Mt 8:20*
  Lu 9:58
v *Mt 8:21*
  Lu 9:59
w *Mt 8:22*
  Lu 9:60

---

1 Gr., *sata*; a measure for dry goods, a *sáton* amounted to roughly twelve litres
2 Verses 37-40 are not found in the best ancient mss.

A storm arises

along, as he was in the boat, and other boats were also with him.ˣ

42 And there arose a great squall;ʸ and the waves were breaking over the boat, so that it was filling with water.ᶻ

43 And he was in the stern, sleeping on the cushion; and they woke him, saying, "Teacher, does it not concern you, that we perish?"ᵃ

44 ³[And having been woken, he rebuked the wind, and said to the sea, "Hush, be quiet!" And the wind abated, and there was a great calm.ᵇ]

45 And he said to them, "Why are you timid? Have you still no faith?"ᶜ

46 ³[But having been afraid, they wondered, saying to one another, "Who is this, then, that he gives orders even to the winds and the water, and they obey him?"ᵈ]

47 And they came to the other side of the sea, into the land of the Gerasenes.ᵉ

48 And having come out of the boat, immediately *there* came out of the tombs to meet him a man with an unclean spirit.ᶠ

---

3 Verses 44 and 46 are not found in the best ancient mss.

x Ps 107:23,24
  Mr 4:36
y Ps 107:25,26
z Jon 1:4
  Mt 8:24
  Mr 4:37
  Lu 8:23
a Ps 107:27,28
  Jon 1:5,6,13
  Mt 8:25
  Mr 4:38
  Lu 8:24
b Ps 107:29
  Mt 8:26
  Mr 4:39
  Lu 8:24
c Ec 3:1,2
  Ec 8:8
  Mr 4:40
d Mt 8:27
  Mr 4:41
  Lu 8:25
e Ps 107:30
  Mt 8:28
  Mr 5:1
  Lu 8:26
f Mt 8:28
  Mr 5:2
  Lu 8:27

5 — The herd of swine

49 And having seen Jesus from a distance, he was crying out with a loud voice, saying, "What have I to do with you? Go away!"[g]

50 For he was saying to him, "Come forth, *you* unclean spirit!"[h]

51 Now near the mountain, there was a large herd of swine grazing;[i] and immediately the herd rushed down the steep bank into the sea.[4][j]

52 And those who fed them fled, and reported it to the city; and they went out to see what it was that had happened.[k]

53 And they came to Jesus,[l] and those who had seen it related to them how it happened to the one possessed by demons, and about the swine.[m]

54 And they began to implore him to go away from their region.[n]

55 And having gotten into the boat, the man with the unclean spirit was admonishing him, that he might be with him.[o]

56 And he did not let him, but sent him away.[p]

---

[g] Mt 8:29; Mr 5:7; Lu 8:28
[h] Mr 5:8; Lu 8:29
[i] Mt 8:30; Mr 5:11; Lu 8:32
[j] Mt 8:32; Mr 5:13; Lu 8:33
[k] Mt 8:33; Mr 5:14; Lu 8:34,35
[l] Mt 8:34; Mr 5:15
[m] Mr 5:16; Lu 8:36
[n] Mt 8:34; Mr 5:17; Lu 8:37
[o] Mr 5:18; Lu 8:38
[p] Mr 5:19; Lu 8:38

4 Certain later mss. add, *about two hundred, and they were drowned in the sea*

Chapter 6

AND when Jesus had again crossed over to the other side,[a] a great crowd gathered around him, and he was by the sea.[b]

2 But some of them were saying, "By Beelzebul, the ruler of the demons, he casts out the demons."[c]

3 And having called them to himself, he was saying to them in parables,[d] "How can Satan cast out Satan?[e]

4 "And if a kingdom[f] is divided against itself,[g] that kingdom is not able to stand.[h]

5 "And if a house is divided against itself,[i] that house is not able to stand.[j]

6 "And if Satan[k] has risen up against himself, and has been divided,[l] he is not able to stand, but has come to an end."[m]

7 And behold, while he was saying these things to them, there came one of the rulers of the synagogue, named Jarius; and having seen him, he fell at his feet,[n]

a Mt 9:1
b Mr 5:21
   Lu 8:40
c Mt 12:24
   Mr 3:22
   Lu 11:15
d Mt 13:34
e Mr 3:23
f Ex 19:5,6
g De 32:20
   Isa 1:2
   Isa 30:9
h Mt 12:25
   Mr 3:24
   Lu 11:17
i Isa 5:1-7
   Jer 11:10,11
   Eze 8:6
   Eze 18:25,29
   Eze 33:20
j Mt 12:25
   Mr 3:25
   Lu 11:17
k 2Sa 24:1
   1Ch 21:1
l Eze 28:2,16
m Eze 28:18,19
   Mt 12:26
   Mr 3:26
   Lu 11:18
n Mt 9:18
   Mr 5:22
   Lu 8:41

8 and he exhorted him much, saying, "My little daughter is extremely *ill*; come and lay the hands on her, that she might be healed and live."°

9 And he departed with him, and a great crowd followed him, and was pressing on him *from all sides*.ᵖ

10 And a woman, being with a flow of blood *for* ¹many years, having heard about Jesus, came in the crowd behind him and touched his cloak.ᵠ

11 For she was saying, "If I shall but touch his outer garments, I will be healed."ʳ

12 And immediately Jesus, knowing in himself that power had gone out of him,ˢ *and* having turned around in the crowd, said, "Who touched my outer garments?"ᵗ

13 And his disciples said to him, "You see the crowd pressing on you *from all sides*, and you say, 'Who touched me?'"ᵘ

14 And he looked around to see who had done this.ᵛ

15 And the woman, having been frightened and trembling, came and fell down before him, and told him all the truth.ʷ

16 And he said to her, "Daughter, your faith has

---

o Mt 9:18
   Mr 5:23
   Lu 8:41
p Mt 9:19
   Mr 5:24
   Lu 8:42
q Mt 9:20
   Mr 5:25,27
   Lu 8:43,44
r Mt 9:21
   Mr 5:28
s Lu 8:46
t Mr 5:30
u Mr 5:31
   Lu 8:45
v Mr 5:32
w Mr 5:33
   Lu 8:47

1 According to the best ancient mss.; most later mss. read, *twelve*

"Your faith has healed you. Go your way."[x]

17 And while he was still speaking, they came from the ruler of the synagogue's *house*, saying, "Your daughter has died. Why do you still trouble the teacher?"[y]

18 But Jesus, disregarding what was spoken, said to the ruler of the synagogue, "Fear not, only have faith."[z]

19 And he allowed no one to follow him; and he came to the ruler of the synagogue's house, and he beheld a commotion, and much weeping and wailing.[a]

20 And entering in, he said to them, "Why do you make a commotion and weep? The child is not dead, but is asleep."[b]

21 And they scorned him. But having put them all out, he took the child's father and mother with him and entered in where the child was.[c]

22 And having taken the child by the hand, he said to her, "Talitha koum."[2][d]

23 And at that moment, the girl got up and walked; and immediately they were greatly bewildered.[e]

24 And he admonished them many *times*, that no one should know *of* it; and he said *something* should be

[x] Mt 9:22
Mr 5:34
Lu 8:48
[y] Mr 5:35
Lu 8:49
[z] Mr 5:36
Lu 8:50
[a] Mt 9:23
Mr 5:37,38
Lu 8:52
[b] Mt 9:24
Mr 5:39
Lu 8:52
[c] Mr 5:40
Lu 8:53
[d] Mt 9:25
Mr 5:41
Lu 8:54
[e] Mt 9:25
Mr 5:42
Lu 8:55,56

---

2 Certain later mss. add, *which is translated, "Little girl, I say to you, arise"*

6   Jairus' daughter recovers   John the Baptist's query

f   *Mr 5:43*
    Lu 8:55,56
g   *Mt 11:2*
    Lu 7:18
h   *Isa 40:3*
    Mal 3:1
    Mal 4:5,6
i   *Lu 7:19*
j   *Mt 11:3*
    Lu 7:20
k   *Isa 32:3,4*
    Lu 7:21
l   *Mt 11:4*
    Lu 7:22
m   *Isa 42:18-20*
    Mt 11:6
    Lu 7:23
n   *1Ki 14:15*
    Mt 11:7
    Lu 7:24

given her to eat.^f

25 And word was brought to John by his disciples, concerning all of these things.^g

26 And having summoned a certain two of his disciples, John sent them to Jesus, saying "Are you the coming one?^h Or should we wait for *someone who is different?*"ⁱ

27 And having come to him, the men said, "John the Baptist has sent us to you, saying 'Are you the coming one? Or should we expect someone else?'"^j

28 At that hour, he was healing many of diseases and afflictions and evil spirits, and to many blind *people*, he showed favor to see.^k

29 And answering, he said to them, "Go, report to John what you have seen and heard,^l and *say*, he is blessed who shall not be offended by me."^m

30 And when John's messengers had departed, he began to speak to the crowds about John. "What have you gone out into the wilderness to gaze at? A reed shaken by *the* wind?ⁿ

31 "But what have you gone out to see? A man dressed in soft clothes? Behold, those who *are dressed* in splendid clothes and *who* are living in luxury are in

One who is least in the kingdom of God is greater than John

palaces.º

32 "But what have you gone out to see? A prophet? Yes, I say to you, and *one* considerably more than a prophet.ᵖ

33 "This is the one of whom it has been written, 'BEHOLD, I SEND MY MESSENGER BEFORE ME, AND HE WILL PREPARE THE WAY BEFORE ME.'ᑫ

34 "I say to you, among those born of women, no one is greater than John; but *one who is* least in the kingdom of God is greater than he.ʳ

35 "The Law and the prophets *were preached* until John.ˢ Since then, the good news of the kingdom of God is proclaimed, and everyone is ardently jostling to get into it.ᵗ

36 "And if you are willing to accept it, he is Elijah, the one who is to come.ᵘ

37 "He who has ears,ᵛ let him hear.ʷ

38 "But to what will I liken this generation? It is like little children sitting in the markets and calling out to others who are different,ˣ

39 saying, 'We played the flute for you, and you did not dance. We lamented for you, and you did not mourn.'ʸ

o 1Ki 7:1-8
   2Ch 9:3,4
   Mt 11:8
   Lu 7:25
p Mt 11:9
   Lu 7:26
q Mal 3:1
   Mt 11:10
   Lu 7:27
r Mt 11:11
   Lu 7:28
s De 31:24-29
   Isa 30:9
   Jer 5:23
   Jer 13:8-11
   Eze 2:4,5,7
   Eze 3:7
   Mal 3:1
t Mt 11:12
   Lu 16:16
u Mal 4:5
   Mt 11:14
v Ex 21:5,6
   De 15:16,17
w Mt 11:15
x Mt 11:16
   Lu 7:31,32
y Mt 11:17
   Lu 7:32

40 "Indeed, John came, neither eating nor drinking, and they say, 'He has a demon!'"ᶻ

41 "The son of man came, eating and drinking, and they say, 'Behold, a man, a glutton and a drinker of wine, a friend of tax collectors and of sinners!'"ᵃ

42 "And the wisdom was justified by her children."ᵇ

43 Now as he was speaking, a Pharisee asked him to dine with him, and having entered, he reclined.ᶜ

44 But the Pharisee wondered, having seen that he had not first washed before the meal.ᵈ

45 But the master said to him, "Now you Pharisees, you cleanse the outside of the cup and the plate, but inside they are full of pillaging and self-indulgence.ᵉ

46 "Blind Pharisee, first make the inside of the cup clean, that the outside of it might also become clean."ᶠ

47 And having summoned the crowd, he said to them, "Hear and understand –ᵍ

48 not that which enters into the mouth defiles the man, but that which comes forth from the mouth, this *is what* defiles the man."ʰ

49 Then, having come near, the disciples said to him, "Do you know that the Pharisees, having heard this speech, were offended?"[i]

50 But he answered, saying, "Leave them alone; they are blind guides who strain out the gnat, but swallow *the* camel.[j] But if a blind guide guides a blind man, both will fall into a pit."[k]

51 But having answered, Simon said to him, "Explain this parable to us."[l]

52 And he said, "Are you also still without understanding?[m]

53 "Do you not yet understand that everything which enters into the mouth goes into the belly, and is made to go out in the privy, making all foods clean?[n]

54 "But the things which go forth out of the mouth come forth out of the heart, and those defile the man.[o]

55 "For out the heart come forth evil thoughts,[3] slaughters, malice, deceit, *the* evil eye, slander, pride, recklessness.[p]

56 "All these evils come forth from within, and defile the man."[q]

57 But having risen up from that place, he went away into the region of Tyre.[r]

---
3 Certain later mss. add, *adulteries, fornications, thefts*

The Canaanite woman

^s Mt 15:22
Mr 7:25,26
^t Mt 15:23
^u Ps 74:1
Jer 12:7
Eze 34:5,6
Mt 9:36
Mt 15:24
Mt 18:11
^v Mt 15:25
^w Mt 15:26
Mr 7:27
^x Ps 45:10-12
Mt 15:27
Mr 7:28
^y Mt 9:22
Mr 5:34
Mr 10:52
Lu 8:48
Lu 18:42
^z Mt 15:28
Mr 7:29,30

58 And behold, a Canaanite woman, having come out from that region, cried out, saying, "Have mercy on me, Master[4] — my daughter is grievously demon-possessed!"[s]

59 But he answered her not a word. And having come near, his disciples solicited him, saying, "Send her away, for she is shouting behind us."[t]

60 But answering, he said, "I was not sent, except to the lost sheep of the house of Israel."[u]

61 But the *woman*, having come, knelt down and kissed *his hand*, saying, "Master, help me!"[v]

62 But answering, he said, "It is not good to take the children's bread and throw it to puppies."[w]

63 But she said, "Master, even puppies eat from the crumbs which fall under their master's table."[x]

64 Then, answering, he said to her, "O woman, great *is* your faith.[y] Be it to you as you wish." And her daughter was healed from that hour.[z]

---

[4] Certain later mss. add, *son of David*

Chapter 7

A<small>ND</small> having departed from there, Jesus went along the sea of Galilee; and having gone up on the mountain, he was sitting there.[a]

2 And it came about, as he was praying in a certain place, that when he ceased, one of his disciples said to him, "Master, teach us to pray, just as John taught his disciples."[b]

3 But he said to them, "When you pray, say, 'Our Father, who *is* in heaven,[1][c]

4 give us today our daily bread.'"[d]

5 And he said to them, "Who among you will have a friend, and will go to him at midnight, and say to him, 'Friend, lend me three loaves of bread,[e]

6 for a friend of mine has come to me on a journey, and I have nothing to set before him.'[f]

7 "And he, answering from within, will say, 'Do

---

a *Mt 15:29*
b *Lu 5:33*
  Lu 11:1
c *Mt 6:9*
  Lu 11:2
d *Pr 30:8*
  Mt 6:11
  Lu 11:3
e *Lu 11:5*
f *Lu 11:6*

---

1 Certain later mss. add, *hallowed be your name*

Good gifts given to those who ask

not cause me trouble! The door has already been shut, and my children are in bed with me. I cannot get up to give you *anything*.'[g]

8 "I say to you, even if he will not get up and give him *anything* on account of being his friend, yet because of his shameless importunity, having *been* woken, he will give him as much as he needs.[h]

9 "And I say to you, ask, and it will be given to you; seek, and you will find; knock, and it will be opened to you.[i]

10 "For everyone who asks, receives; and everyone who seeks, finds; and to everyone who knocks, it will be opened.[j]

11 "But which of you who is a father,[k] to a son who will ask for a loaf of bread, will give him a stone?[l]

12 "Or *who will ask for* a fish, and instead of a fish, will give him a serpent?[m]

13 "Or if he should ask for an egg, will give him a scorpion?[n]

14 "Therefore, if you, being evil,[o] know *how* to give good gifts to your children, how much more will your Father, who *is* in the heavens, give good *gifts* to those who ask Him?"[p]

---

g Pr 3:27,28
  Lu 11:7
h Ps 78:18,21
  Ps 78:23-25,29
  Ps 105:40
  Lu 11:8
i Mt 7:7
  Lu 11:9
j Mt 7:8
  Lu 11:10
k Ex 4:22
l De 9:9-11
  Mt 4:3
  Mt 7:9
m Nu 21:6
  Mt 7:10
  Lu 11:11
n 2Ch 10:11,15
  Lu 11:12
o Ge 6:5
  Ps 53:2,3
  Ec 9:3
  Jer 16:12
p Ps 16:10
  Mt 7:7
  Mt 7:11
  Mt 26:39
  Mt 27:46
  Mr 14:36
  Mr 15:34
  Lu 11:10
  Lu 11:13
  Lu 22:42

Jesus teaches in Nazareth

15 And he went out from there and came into his own country, where he was brought up. And according to his custom, on the day of the Sabbath, he entered into the synagogue and stood up to read.^q

16 And the scroll of the prophet Isaiah was handed to him, and having unrolled the scroll, he found the place where it was written,^r

17   "THE SPIRIT OF THE LORD GOD IS UPON ME,
   BECAUSE GOD HAS ANOINTED ME
   TO BRING GOOD NEWS TO THE MEEK;
   TO BIND UP THE CRUSHED,^s
   TO PROCLAIM RELEASE TO THE CAPTIVES
   AND FREEDOM TO THE BOUND."^t

18 And having rolled up the scroll and given it back to the attendant, he sat down, and all eyes in the synagogue were staring at him.^u

19 And he began to say to them, "Today this Scripture is fulfilled in your ears."^v

20 And many *of those* listening were astounded, saying, "From where *do* these things *come* to him, and what *is* the wisdom that has been given to him, and do such works of power come about by his hands?^w

21 "Is this not the carpenter, the son of Mary, and *the* brother of James, and Joses, and Judas, and

q Mt 13:54
   Mr 6:1,2
   Lu 4:16
r Lu 4:17
s Le 26:14-19
   De 7:9,10
   Jer 19:1-11
   La 3:1-16
t Le 25:55
   Isa 44:21
   Isa 61:1
   Ho 10:10
   Lu 4:18
u Lu 4:20
v Isa 42:1,5-7
   Lu 4:21
w Isa 40:14
   Mt 13:54
   Mr 6:2

7   Jesus sends out the disciples in pairs

<small>
x   Mt 13:55,56
     Mr 6:3
y   De 13:1,3,5
     Jer 23:16
     Mr 6:3
z   Mt 13:57
     Mr 6:4
     Lu 4:24
     Jn 4:44
a   Mt 13:58
     Mr 6:5
b   Mt 9:22
     Mr 5:34
     Mr 5:36
     Mr 10:52
     Lu 8:48
     Lu 8:50
     Lu 17:19
     Lu 18:42
c   Mr 6:6
d   Mt 10:5
     Mr 6:7
     Lu 9:1
e   Mt 10:7
     Lu 9:2
f   Mt 10:9
     Mr 6:8
     Lu 9:3
     Lu 22:35
g   Mt 10:10
     Mr 6:9
     Lu 9:3
h   Mt 10:11
     Mr 6:10
     Lu 9:4
</small>

Simon? And are not his sisters here with us?"[x]

22 And they took offense at him.[y] But he said to them, "A prophet is not without honor, except in his own country, among his own relatives and in his own house."[z]

23 And he was not able to do there any work of power, except for a few sick people he healed, having laid the hands on *them*.[a]

24 And he wondered at their lack of faith.[b] And he went about the surrounding villages, teaching.[c]

25 And summoning the twelve, he began to send them out two *by* two, and he gave them authority *over* the unclean spirits,[d]

26 and he sent them to proclaim the kingdom of God, and to heal the sick.[e]

27 And he said to them, "Take nothing for the journey, except a staff only — neither bread nor bag nor money in the belt —[f]

28 but *go* wearing sandals, and do not put on two tunics."[g]

29 And he said to them, "Wherever you enter into a house, stay there until you go out from there.[h]

30 "And any place that will not receive you, not even

hear you, going out from there, shake off the dust which *is* under your feet, as a testimony for them." ⁱ

31 And going out, they passed through the villages, announcing *the* good news and healing everywhere.ʲ

32 Now ²Herod the tetrarch heard of all the things being done, and was perplexed, because it was said by some that John had been raised from among *the* dead;ᵏ

33 but by some, that Elijah had appeared; but by others that a prophet, one of the ancients, had arisen.ˡ

34 But Herod said, "John, I beheaded. But who is this, about whom I hear such *things*?"ᵐ

35 ³[For Herod himself, having sent *soldiers,* seized John and bound him in prison on account of Herodias, the wife of his brother Philip, because he had married her.ⁿ

36 Yet John was saying to Herod, "It is not lawful for you to have your brother's wife."ᵒ

37 And Herodias held it against him and wanted to kill him, and *yet* was not able *to*;ᵖ for Herod feared the multitude, because they held John to be a prophet.ᑫ

38 And an opportune day came, when Herod on

i Isa 52:2
  Mt 10:14
  Mr 6:11
  Lu 9:5
j Lu 9:6
k Mt 14:1
  Mr 6:14
  Lu 9:7
l Mt 16:14
  Mr 6:15
  Lu 9:8
m Lu 9:9
n Mt 14:3
  Mr 6:17
  Lu 3:20
o Le 18:16
  Le 20:21
  Mt 14:4
  Mr 6:18
  Lu 3:19
p Mr 6:19
q De 18:15,18
  Mt 14:5
  Mt 21:26
  Mr 11:32
  Lu 20:6

---

2 Herod Antipas, tetrarch of Galilee and Perea from 4 BCE – 39 CE, and son of Herod the Great
3 Verses 35-46 are not found in the best ancient mss.

John the Baptist is beheaded

his birthday gave a banquet for lords, and his military commanders, and the notables of Galilee;[r]

39 and the daughter of he *and* Herodias having come in, and having danced, she pleased Herod and his guests, and the king said to the girl, "Ask *of* me whatever you want, and I will give *it* to you."[s]

40 And he swore to her, "Whatever you might ask of me, I will give to you, up to half of my kingdom."[t]

41 And having gone out, she said to her mother, "What shall I ask *for*?" And she said, "The head of John the Baptist."[u]

42 And having entered in immediately with haste before the king, she asked, saying, "I want that you at once give to me the head of John the Baptist on a platter."[v]

43 And although the king was greatly grieved, on account of the oaths *he had made* and his guests, he would not annul it.[w]

44 And immediately the king sent an executioner, and commanded that his head be brought; and he went and beheaded him in the prison,[x]

45 and brought the head upon a platter, and gave it to the girl, and the girl gave it to her mother.[y]

---

r Mr 6:21
s Mt 14:6,7
  Mr 6:22
t Mr 6:23
u Mt 14:8
  Mr 6:24
v Mt 14:8
  Mr 6:25
w Mt 14:9
  Mr 6:26
x Mt 14:10
  Mr 6:27
y Mt 14:11
  Mr 6:28

Jesus and the disciples withdraw to a solitary place

46 And having heard *of it*, his disciples came and took away the corpse and laid it in a tomb.[z]]

47 And having returned, the disciples related to him how much they had done.[a]

48 And he said to them, "Come away by yourselves to a solitary place, and rest a little while." For there were many who were coming and who were going, and they did not even have time to eat.[b]

49 So they went away in the boat to a solitary place by themselves.[c]

50 And *many* saw them going, and recognized *them*, and *they* ran there together on foot from all the towns and went before them.[d]

51 And having gone out *of the boat*, he saw *a* great crowd, and he was moved with compassion for them, for they were like sheep without a shepherd;[e] and he began to teach them many things.[f]

52 And already the hour having become much, the disciples, having come to him, said, "The place is desolate, and the hour *is* already much;[g]

53 send them away, that having gone to the surrounding farms and villages, they might buy for themselves something to eat."[h]

z Mt 14:12
  Mr 6:29
a Mr 6:30
  Lu 9:10
b Mr 6:31
c Mt 14:13
  Mr 6:32
  Jn 6:1
d Mt 14:13
  Mr 6:33
  Lu 9:11
  Jn 6:2
e Ps 23:1
  Ps 44:9-22
  Ps 74:1
  Ps 78:52
  Ps 80:1
  Jer 12:7
  Eze 34:4-6
  Mt 9:36
  Jn 10:11
f Mr 6:34
  Lu 9:11
g Mt 14:15
  Mr 6:35
  Lu 9:12
h Mt 14:15
  Mr 6:36
  Lu 9:12

7 The crowd comes to Jesus and is fed

ⁱ Mt 14:16
Mr 6:37
Lu 9:13
^j Mt 14:17
Mr 6:38
Lu 9:13
^k Mt 14:18
Lu 11:5,6
^l Mt 6:9,11
Mt 7:11
^m Mt 14:19
Mr 6:41
Lu 9:16
Jn 6:11
ⁿ Mt 14:20
Mr 6:42
Lu 9:17
^o Mt 14:20
Mr 6:43
Lu 9:17
Jn 6:13
^p Mt 14:21
Mr 6:44
Lu 9:14
Jn 6:10
^q Mt 14:22
Mr 6:45
^r Mt 14:23
Mr 6:46

54 But Jesus said to them, "They have no need to go away — you give them *something* to eat!"[i]

55 But they said to him, "We have nothing here, except [4]three loaves and a few small fish."[j]

56 But he said, "Bring them to me here."[k]

57 And having ordered the crowds to sit down on the grass, having taken the [4]loaves, having looked up to heaven,[l] he blessed *the loaves*; and having broken *them*, he gave the loaves to the disciples, and the disciples *gave them* to the crowds.[m]

58 And all ate and were satisfied.[n]

59 [5][And they picked up the broken pieces that were left over, twelve baskets full.[o]

60 But those who were eating were about five thousand men, besides women and children.[p]]

61 And immediately, he compelled his disciples to enter into the boat, and to go ahead to the other side, until he should dismiss the crowds.[q]

62 And having dismissed the crowds, he went up by himself on the mountain to pray.[r]

63 And evening having come, the boat was in the

---

4 According to the best ancient mss.; later mss. read, *five loaves and two fish*
5 Verses 59 and 60 are not found in the best ancient mss.

50   *The Gospel of Jesus of Nazareth*

From their boat, the disciples see Jesus

midst of the sea, and he was alone upon the land.^s

64 And having seen them, he came towards them, walking near the sea.^t

65 And having seen him walking near the sea, they thought that he was a ghost, and they cried out.^u

66 For *the disciples* all saw him, and were troubled. But immediately he spoke with them, and he said to them, "Be of good cheer, fear not!"^v

67 And having come out of their boat, and having immediately recognized him,^w

68 then they were willing to receive him into the boat. And immediately the boat was at the land to which they were going.^x

69 And having crossed over to the land, they came to Gennesaret, and moored *at the shore*.^y

70 Now as they went *along*, he entered into a certain village, and a certain woman named Martha received him.^z

71 And she had a sister called Mary, and *who*, having sat down at the master's feet, was listening to his word.^a

72 But Martha was greatly troubled about *so* much serving; and confronting him, she said, "Master, is it

s *Mt 14:24*
   Mr 6:47
   Jn 6:17
t *Mt 14:25*
   Mr 6:48
u *Mt 14:26*
   Mr 6:49
   Jn 6:19
v *La 3:57*
   Mt 14:27
   Mr 6:50
   Jn 6:20
w *Mt 14:34*
   Mr 6:54
x *Mr 8:10*
   Jn 6:21
y *Mt 14:34*
   Mr 6:53
   Mr 8:10
z *Lu 10:38*
a *Lu 10:39*

The Gospel of Jesus of Nazareth

of no concern to you, that my sister has left me to serve *all* alone? Speak to her, therefore, that she might help me!"[z]

73 But answering, he said to her, "Martha, Martha, you are anxious and greatly disturbed about *so* much.[a]

74 "But one is necessary, or one Mary — indeed, the good part — chose, which will not be taken from her."[b]

Chapter 8

AND the Pharisees, having come to him, testing *him*, asked him to show them a sign from heaven.[a]

2 But answering, he said to them, "When evening has come, you say, 'Fair weather, for the sky is red.'[b]

3 "And at dawn, 'A storm today, for the sky is red.' Truly, you have learned how to distinguish the face of the sky, but the signs of the appointed times, you are not able."[c]

4 But having been questioned by the Pharisees *as to* when the kingdom of God would come, he

Beware of the leaven of the Pharisees 8

answered them and said, "The kingdom of God does not come with observation.^d

5 "Nor will they say, 'Behold, *it is* here, or there.' For behold, the kingdom of God is within you."^e

6 And having left them, *and* having embarked again, he went away to the other side.^f

7 And they forgot to take bread, and except for one loaf, they had none with them in the boat.^g

8 And he enjoined them, saying, "Behold! Take heed of the leaven of the Pharisees, and the leaven of Herod."^h

9 And they debated with one another, because they did not have bread.ⁱ

10 And realizing this, he said to them, "Why do you debate because you have no bread?^j

11 "How *is it that* you do not understand that I was speaking to you not about bread, but to beware of the leaven of the Pharisees?"^k

12 Then they understood that he had not said to beware of the leaven of bread, but of the teaching of the Pharisees.^l

13 And they came to Bethsaida. And they brought him a blind man, and exhorted him, so that he might

d Joe 2:30,31
  Mic 7:15
  Lu 17:20
e Ps 82:6
  Lu 17:21
  Jn 10:33,34
f Mr 8:13
g Mt 16:5
  Mr 8:14
h Jer 32:21
  Da 4:3
  Da 6:27
  Mt 16:1
  Mt 16:6
  Mr 8:15
  Lu 23:8
i Mt 16:7
  Mr 8:16
j Mt 16:8
  Mr 8:17
k Mt 16:11
l Mt 16:12

The Gospel of Jesus of Nazareth

touch him.ᵐ

14 And having taken hold of the blind man's hand, he led him forth out of the village; and having spat upon his eyes, *and* having laid the hands upon him, he asked him, "Do you see anything?"ⁿ

15 And having looked up, he said, "I see the men, because as trees I see *them*, walking."ᵒ

16 Then he again laid the hands upon his eyes; and he opened his eyes and was restored, and saw all clearly.ᵖ

17 And he sent him to his home, saying, "Do not enter the village, nor tell *it* to anyone in the village."ᑫ

18 And Jesus and his disciples went forth into the villages of Caesarea Philippi; and on the way, he was questioning his disciples, saying to them, "Who do men say me to be?"ʳ

19 But they spoke to him, saying, "John the Baptist; and others, Elijah;ˢ but others, one of the prophets."ᵗ

20 And he questioned them, "But you, who do you say me to be?"ᵘ

21 But Simon answered, saying, "You are the ¹messiah."ᵛ

22 And he sternly told them that they should tell

Jesus rebukes Simon

no one this, that he was the ¹messiah.ʷ

23 And he began to teach them that it was necessary for him to go away to Jerusalem, and to suffer many things from the elders and the chief priests and the scribes, and to be put to death and ²to be raised up.ˣ

24 And he spoke the word forthrightly. And Simon, having taken him aside, began to rebuke him,ʸ saying, "*God be* merciful to you, Master!ᶻ This will never happen to you!"ᵃ

25 But having turned around, and having seen his disciples, he rebuked Simon, and said, "Get behind me, ³Cephas!ᵇ You are a stumbling block to me! For you are not thinking *about* the things of God, but the things of men."ᶜ

26 But he said to his disciples, "It is impossible that stumbling blocks should not come, but woe *to him* by whom they come."ᵈ

27 And having summoned the crowd with his disciples, he said to them, "Truly I say to you, unless you eat the flesh of the son of man, and drink his

w Ps 146:3,4
   Mt 16:20
   Mr 8:30
   Lu 9:21
x Ge 22:2-4
   De 21:22,23
   Ps 25:1
   Mt 16:21
   Mr 8:31
   Lu 9:22
   Jn 8:36
   Jn 12:32
y Mr 8:32
z Ge 22:8,13,14
a De 12:31
   Mt 16:22
b De 32:4
   Jos 24:27
   Ps 18:31
   Jn 1:42
c Mt 16:23
   Mr 8:33
d Mt 18:7
   Lu 17:1

---

1 Gr., *messias*, for the Hebrew *mashiach*; certain later mss. read, *christos*
2 Certain later mss. add, *after three days*
3 Gr., *Képhas*; lit., *stone*; certain mss. read, *Satana*, or Satan

Many of Jesus' disciples withdraw

blood,[e] you have no life in yourselves.[f]

28 "For whoever might wish to save his soul[g] shall lose it, but whoever will lose his soul[h] on account of me shall save it.[i]

29 "For what shall it profit a man if he should gain the whole world,[j] and *yet* forfeit his soul?[k]

30 "For what shall a man give in exchange for his soul?"[l]

31 Then many of his disciples, having heard, were saying, "This is a hard word. Who can listen to it?"[m]

32 But Jesus, knowing in himself that his disciples were grumbling about this, said to them, "Does this cause you to stumble?"[n]

33 And because of this, many of his disciples withdrew and were no longer walking with him.[o]

34 Jesus was therefore saying to those *who were* Jewish *who had* believed him, "If you abide in my word, *then* you are truly my disciples,[p]

35 and you will know the truth, and the truth will [4]set you free."[q]

36 But it came to pass, about eight days after *saying these words, that* Jesus, having taken *with him* Simon

---
4 Or, *liberate you*

e Le 3:17
  Le 17:10
f Mr 9:50
  Lu 12:57
  Jn 6:53
g Le 18:5
  De 30:19,20
  De 32:46,47
h Le 7:25,27
  Le 17:10,14
  Eze 18:4
i Mt 16:25
  Mr 8:35
  Lu 9:24
  Jn 12:47
j Ge 13:14,15
  Ge 17:6-8
  De 11:22-24
  Jos 1:3
k De 6:5
  De 10:12
  De 26:16
  De 30:6
  Mt 16:26
  Mr 8:36
  Lu 9:25
l Le 17:11
  Ps 49:8
  Mt 16:26
  Mr 8:37
  Mr 10:45
  Jn 15:13
m De 13:3,4
  Jn 6:60
n Nu 15:30,31
  Jn 6:61
o Jn 6:66
p Jn 8:31
q Isa 14:12-17
  Eze 28:18,19
  Jn 8:32

Jesus brings Simon, John and James to a high mountain

and John and James, brought them up to a high mountain by themselves.[r]

37 And it came to pass, that the appearance of his face was different,[s] and his clothing gleamed white.[t]

38 And behold, two men were talking with him, who were Moses and Elijah,[u]

39 who, having appeared in glory, were speaking of his exodus, which he was about to fulfill in Jerusalem.[v]

40 Now Simon and those who were with him were heavy with sleep;[w] and he came and found them sleeping, and he said, "Simon, are you asleep?"[x]

41 And answering, Simon said to Jesus, "Rabbi, it is good for us to be here; and let us make three tabernacles, one for you, and one for Moses, and one for Elijah."[y]

42 For he knew not what he should answer.[z]

43 But as he was saying these things, a cloud came, overshadowing them;[a] but they were terrified as they entered into the cloud.[b]

44 And a voice came out of the cloud,[c] "This is my beloved son.[d] Listen to him!"[e]

45 And having heard, the disciples fell upon their faces, and were frightened out of their wits.[f]

r Ps 89:12
　Isa 40:9
　Na 1:15
　Mt 17:1
　Mr 9:2
　Lu 9:28
s Ex 34:29,35
t Mt 17:2
　Mr 9:3
　Lu 9:29
u Am 3:3
　Mt 17:3
　Mr 9:4
　Lu 9:30
v Mr 9:31
　Mr 10:33,34
　Lu 9:31
　Lu 9:44
w Lu 9:32
x Mr 14:37,40
y Mt 17:4
　Mr 9:5
　Lu 9:33
z Mr 9:6
a Ex 24:15,16
　Mt 17:5
　Mr 9:7
b Lu 9:34
c Ex 19:9
d Ge 22:2
　Ps 2:7
e Mt 17:5
　Mr 9:7
　Lu 9:34,35
f Ge 17:3
　Nu 20:6
　1Ki 18:39
　Mt 17:6

The Gospel of Jesus of Nazareth

46 And Jesus, having come near, and having touched them, said, "Rise up, and do not be afraid."[g]

47 And suddenly, having looked around, they no longer saw anyone with themselves, except Jesus.[h]

48 And as they were coming down the mountain, he ordered them that they should tell no one what they had seen.[i]

CHAPTER 9

AND it came to pass the next day, when they had come down from the mountain, that he saw a great crowd, and *some* scribes disputing with them.[a]

2 And immediately, having seen him, they were astounded, and running to him, they greeted him. And he asked them, "What are you disputing with them?"[b]

3 And they brought a woman who had been caught in adultery, and having stood her in the midst,[c]

4 they said to him, "Teacher, this woman was caught in the very act of committing adultery.[d]

"Neither do I condemn you"

5 "Now in the Law, Moses commanded *that* such *a woman* be stoned;[e] what say you, therefore?"[f]

6 But Jesus, having stooped down, with *his* finger wrote on the ground.[g]

7 Yet as they continued to ask him, having straightened himself up, he said to them, "The one among you who is without sin,[h] let him cast the first stone at her."[i]

8 And again, having stooped down, he wrote on the ground.[j]

9 But having heard *this*, they went out, one by one, beginning with the older men, and he was left alone, and the woman was in the midst.[k]

10 And having straightened up, Jesus said to her, "Woman, where are they? Has no one condemned you?"[l]

11 And she said, "No one, sir." And Jesus said to her, "Neither do I condemn you. Go in peace."[m]

12 And behold, a man from the crowd cried out, saying, "Master, I implore you, look upon my son, for he is ¹epileptic."[n]

13 "And behold, a spirit takes him, and suddenly

---

1 Lit., *moonstruck*

e De 22:23,24
f Jn 8:5
g Ex 24:12
  Ex 31:18
  Jn 8:6
h Ex 20:14
  Lu 1:28-31
  Lu 1:34,35,38
  Lu 6:41
i De 17:7
  Jn 8:7
j Mt 7:1
  Jn 8:8
k Jn 8:9
l Pr 20:9
  Ec 7:20
  Jn 8:10
m Jn 8:11
  Jn 8:15
n Mt 17:14,15
  Mr 9:17
  Lu 9:38

o	Mr 9:18 Lu 9:39
p	Mt 17:16 Mr 9:18 Lu 9:40
q	Mt 17:17 Mr 9:19 Lu 9:41
r	Mr 9:20 Lu 9:42
s	Mr 9:21
t	Mr 9:22
u	Mt 17:18 Mr 9:25 Lu 9:42
v	Mr 9:26
w	Mr 9:27

he cries out, and it throws him into convulsions, with foaming *at the mouth*; and *it* departs from him with difficulty, and *it* batters him.º

14 "And I brought him to your disciples, and they were not able to heal him."ᵖ

15 And answering, he said, "Bring me to him."ᑫ

16 And they brought him to him. And immediately, the spirit threw him into convulsions, and having fallen upon the ground, he rolled *about* and foamed *at the mouth*.ʳ

17 And he asked his father, "How long has it been this way with him?" And he said, "Since childhood,ˢ

18 and *it happens* often, and it casts him into the fire, and into the waters, that it might destroy him. But if you are able to do anything, help us, have pity on us!"ᵗ

19 But Jesus, having seen that a crowd was rapidly gathering, rebuked the unclean spirit.ᵘ

20 And having cried out and thrown him into many convulsions, it came out; and he became as if dead, so that many said that he was dying.ᵛ

21 But Jesus, having taken him by the hand, raised him up, and he arose.ʷ

22 And having entered into a house, his disciples

The temple tax

asked him in private, "Why were we not able to cast it out?"[x]

23 And he said to them, "This kind can *be made to come out by nothing, except by prayer.*"[y]

24 And from there, having gone forth, they passed through Galilee, and he did not want that anyone should know,[z]

25 for he was teaching his disciples, and was saying to them, "The son of man is to be delivered into *the* hands of men; and they will kill him and [2]he will be raised up."[a]

26 But they did not understand the statement, and they were afraid to ask him.[b]

27 Now when they had come to Capernaum, those who receive the [3]didrachma approached Simon and said, "Does your teacher not pay the didrachma?"[c]

28 He said, "Yes." And when he had come into the house, Jesus anticipated him, saying, "What do you think, Simon? The kings of the earth,[d] from whom do they receive customs or poll-tax? From their sons,[e] or from strangers?"[f]

---

x Mt 17:19
　Mr 9:28
y Mt 17:21
　Mr 9:29
z Mr 9:30
a Mt 17:22,23
　Mt 26:45-47
　Mt 27:22,26,31
　Mr 9:31
　Mr 14:41-43
　Mr 15:10,13,15
　Lu 9:44
b Mr 9:32
　Lu 9:45
c Ex 30:12-16
　Mt 17:24
d Ps 24:1,10
　Ps 47:2
　Ps 103:19
e Ex 4:22
　Ex 6:5-7
　De 14:1,2
　Ps 82:6
　Jer 3:19
　Ho 11:1
f Le 25:23
　Le 25:39,40,42
　Le 25:55
　1Ch 29:15
　Job 41:4
　Ps 39:12
　Isa 44:21
　Mt 17:25

---

2 Certain later mss. add, *on the third day*
3 A Greek coin, the didrachm was equivalent to half a Tyrian shekel, and paid as a temple tax

9   "The one who wishes to become great will be your servant"

29 But he having said, "From strangers", Jesus said to him, "Therefore, the sons are [4]free.[g]

30 "But so that we might not offend them, having gone to the sea, cast *in* a hook, and take the first fish having come up; and having opened its mouth, you will find a [5]stater. Having taken that, give *that* to them for me and you."[h]

31 And in the house, it happened *that* he asked them, "What were you debating on the way?"[i]

32 But they kept silent, for on the way, they had been debating with one another who *was* greatest.[j]

33 And having sat down, he called the twelve and said to them, "If anyone wishes to be first, he will be last of all, and servant of all.[k]

34 "You know that those who suppose they rule over the nations[l] subjugate them,[m] and those *who are* their great ones have power over them.[n]

35 "But it shall not be so among you; however, the one who wishes to become great among you will be your servant.[o]

36 "For who is greater — the *one* that reclines at

Margin references:
g Mt 17:26
h Mt 17:27
i Mr 9:33
j Mt 18:1
  Mr 9:34
  Lu 9:46
  Lu 22:24
k Mt 19:30
  Mr 3:19
  Mr 9:35
  Jn 13:26-30
l 1Ch 29:11
  2Ch 20:6
  Ps 22:28
  Ps 47:8
m Le 25:55
  De 28:48
  Jer 27:8
n Ge 45:8
  De 5:1
  Jos 1:16-18
  2Sa 22:44,45
  Ps 2:8,9
  Ps 18:43,44
  Mt 20:25
  Mr 10:42
o Mt 20:26
  Mt 23:11
  Mr 10:43

---

4 Or, *unbound*; i.e., not a slave
5 A Greek coin, the stater was equivalent to a Tyrian shekel, itself equivalent to a tetradrachm and used for the payment of the temple tax

A sinful woman anoints Jesus' feet

table, or the *one* that serves? *Is it* not he that reclines at table? But I am in your midst, as the *one* that serves.ᵖ

37 "For the son of man did not come to be served, but to serve, and to give his ⁶life as a ransom for many."ᑫ

38 Now one of the ⁷Pharisees asked him, so that he should eat with him, and having entered into the ⁸Pharisee's house, he reclined *at table*.ʳ

39 And behold, *there was* a woman, who was *such a one as* in the city, a sinner; and having learned that he had reclined *at table*, and having brought an alabaster phial of ointment — ˢ

40 and having stood behind him, at his feet, weeping — *with* tears began to wet his feet, and with the hair of her head was wiping *them*; and *she* was kissing his feet, and was anointing *them* with the ointment.ᵗ

41 But having seen this, the *one* having invited him spoke within himself, saying, "If this were a prophet, he would have known who and what kind of woman touches him, for she is a sinner."ᵘ

42 And answering, Jesus said to him, "Simon, I

p Lu 22:27
q Ex 4:22
  Le 25:55
  Ps 25:1
  Ps 49:6-8
  Ps 106:10
  Mt 20:28
  Mr 10:45
  Jn 8:36
  Jn 15:13
r Lu 7:36
s Lu 7:37
t Lu 7:38
u Eze 16:25,32-34
  Eze 23:45
  Lu 7:39

---

6 Or, *soul*
7 Certain early mss. read, *disciples*
8 Certain early mss. read, *disciple's*

"He to whom little is forgiven, loves little"

^v Lu 7:40
^w Lu 7:41
^x Lu 7:42
^y Lu 7:43
^z Lu 7:44
^a Isa 26:5,6
  Lu 7:45
^b Ec 9:8
^c Lu 7:46
^d De 5:9
  De 29:14-21
  Jos 24:19
  Job 7:21
  Job 10:14
  La 3:42,43
  Ho 1:6
^e 1Sa 8:7
  Ps 78:40
  Isa 9:13
  Jer 5:3,7,9,23
  Am 4:6-11
  Hag 2:17
  Lu 7:47

have something to say to you." And he said, "Say it, Teacher."^v

43 "A certain moneylender had two debtors: one owed *him* five hundred [9]denarii, and *the* other, fifty.^w

44 "They not having the means to repay *their debt*, he forgave them both. Which of them therefore will love him most?"^x

45 Answering, Simon said, "I suppose the one to whom he forgave the most." And he said to him, "Rightly have you judged."^y

46 And having turned to the woman, he said to Simon, "Do you see this woman? I came into your house. You gave me no water for my feet, but she has wet my feet with her tears, and wiped *them* with her hair.^z

47 "You did not give me a kiss, but she, from *the time* that I came in, has not ceased kissing my feet.^a

48 "You did not anoint my head with olive oil,^b but she anointed my feet with ointment.^c

49 "On account of this I say to you, her many sins have been forgiven, for she loved much. On the other hand, *he* to whom little is forgiven,^d loves little."^e

---
[9] A Roman coin, the denarius was equivalent to the wages for a day's work

Chapter 10

AND having risen up from there, he came into the region of Judea, and beyond the Jordan. And crowds were again journeying together with him, and again, as he had been accustomed, he was teaching them.[a]

2 And having come to him, *some* Pharisees questioned him, whether it is lawful for a husband [1]to divorce a wife, testing him.[b]

3 But he answering, said to them, "What did Moses command you?"[c]

4 But they said, "Moses allowed a certificate of divorce to be written, and [1]to divorce *her*."[d]

5 But Jesus said to them, "For your hardness of heart, he wrote this commandment for you.[e]

6 "But since *the* beginning of creation, he made them MALE AND FEMALE.[f]

7 "'FOR THIS A MAN WILL LEAVE HIS FATHER

---
1 Or, *to send away*

a Mt 19:1
  Mr 10:1
b Mt 19:3
  Mr 10:2
c Mr 10:3
d De 24:1
  Mt 1:19
  Mt 5:31
  Mt 19:7
  Mr 10:4
e Mal 2:14-16
  Mt 19:8
  Mr 10:5
f Ge 1:27
  Mt 19:4,8
  Mr 10:6

AND MOTHER, AND SHALL CLEAVE TO HIS WIFE;[g]

8 AND THE TWO WILL BECOME ONE FLESH' — so that they are no longer two, but one flesh.[h]

9 "What God has therefore yoked together, *let* man not separate."[i]

10 And in the house, the disciples again asked him about this.[j]

11 And he said to them, "Whoever [2]divorces his wife[k] and should marry another,[l] commits adultery against her; and whoever might marry[m] *a woman* who is divorced[n] commits adultery."[o]

12 His disciples said to him, "If this is the case of the man with the woman, it is better not to marry!"[p]

13 But he said to them, "Not all *men* make room for this statement, but those to whom it has been given."[q]

14 And they were bringing little children to him, that he might touch them. But *the* disciples rebuked them.[r]

15 But having seen *this*, Jesus was indignant, and said to them, "Permit the little children to come to me. Do not hinder them, for the kingdom of God is such *as they*.[s]

---

2 Or, *sends away*

Receive the kingdom of God like a child   10

16 "Truly I say to you, whoever shall not ³receive the kingdom of God as *he receives* a child, shall never enter into it."[t]

17 And having taken them in his arms, he blessed them, having laid the hands on them.[u]

18 And *he* going forth on his way, one having run up and having fallen on his knees before him asked him, "Good Teacher, what shall I do, so that I might inherit eternal life?"[v]

19 But Jesus said to him, "Why do you call me good?[w] No one *is* good, except one – God.[x]

20 "You know the commandments: YOU SHOULD NOT MURDER. YOU SHOULD NOT COMMIT ADULTERY. YOU SHOULD NOT STEAL. YOU SHOULD NOT BEAR FALSE WITNESS. HONOR YOUR FATHER AND YOUR MOTHER."[y]

21 But he said, "Teacher, all these I have kept from *my* youth."[z]

22 But Jesus, having looked upon him, loved him, and said to him, "One thing to you is lacking. Go, sell whatever you have, and give to the poor, and you will have treasure in heaven. And come, follow me!"[a]

---
3 Or, *welcome*

t Mr 10:15
   Lu 18:17
u Mr 10:16
v Job 33:28
   Ps 16:10,11
   Ps 21:2,4
   Isa 25:7-9
   Mt 19:16
   Mr 10:17
   Lu 10:25
   Lu 18:18
w Ge 1:4
   Ec 11:7
   Jn 1:4
   Jn 9:5
x Am 5:18,20
   Mt 19:17
   Mr 10:18
   Lu 18:19
y De 4:40
   De 30:15-20
   De 32:47
   Eze 18:9
   Mt 19:17-19
   Mr 10:19
   Lu 18:20
z Mt 19:20
   Mr 10:20
   Lu 18:21
a Pr 23:4,5
   Ec 7:11
   Jn 8:12
   Mt 19:21
   Mr 10:21
   Lu 18:22

Parable of the rich man

b Pr 18:11
Mt 19:22
Mr 10:22
Lu 18:23
c Mt 19:23
Mr 10:23
Lu 18:24
d Mt 10:9
Mt 19:23
Mr 10:24
Lu 6:20
Lu 22:35
e Mt 19:24
Mr 10:25
Lu 18:25
f Mt 19:25
Mr 10:26
Lu 18:26
g Pr 3:10
Lu 12:16
h Lu 12:17
i Lu 12:18

23 But the *man*, having been saddened by the word, went away vexed, for he had many possessions.[b]

24 But Jesus, having seen him, said, "How hard shall *it be for* those having riches to enter into the kingdom of God."[c]

25 Now the disciples were astonished by his words. But Jesus, having answered again, said to them, "Children, how difficult it is, to enter into the kingdom of God.[d]

26 "It is easier *for* a camel to pass through the eye of a needle, than *for* a rich man to enter into the kingdom of God."[e]

27 But they were exceedingly thunderstruck, saying among themselves, "And who is able to be saved?"[f]

28 But he told them a parable, saying, "The field of a certain rich man brought *forth* a good harvest.[g]

29 "And he was reasoning within himself, saying, 'What shall I do? For I have no place where I may gather together *all of* my fruits.'[h]

30 "And he said, 'I will do this: I will pull down my granaries and I will build larger ones, and there I will gather together all of my grain and my goods.[i]

31 "'And I will say to my soul, "Soul, you have

many good *things* laid up for years — take your ease, eat, drink, *and* be of good cheer!'"ʲ

32 "But God said to him, 'Fool! This night, they demand back your soul.ᵏ But what you prepared, to whom will *it* be?'"ˡ

33 And he said to his disciples, "Through this, I say to you, do not be anxious for *your* life, what you should eat, nor for your body, what you should put on.ᵐ

34 "For life is more than food, and the body *more than* clothing.ⁿ

35 "Consider the ravens, since they neither sow nor reap, for whom there is no granary nor storeroom; and God feeds them.ᵒ How much more different are you than the birds!ᵖ

36 "But which of you, being anxious, is able to add a cubit to his ⁴lifespan?ᑫ

37 "Therefore, if you are not able *to do* even a very little thing, why are you anxious about the rest?ʳ

38 "Consider the lilies, how they grow: they neither toil nor spin — but I say to you, not even Solomon in all his glory was clothed as one of these.ˢ

39 "But if God so clothes the grass — which is in

---
4 Or, *stature*

j Lu 12:19
k Ps 90:3
   Ps 104:29
   Ec 12:7
l Ps 39:5,6
   Ec 2:21
   Lu 12:20
m Mt 6:25
   Lu 12:22
n Mt 6:25
   Lu 12:23
o Ps 104:27,28
   Ps 136:25
   Ps 147:9
p Mt 6:26
   Lu 12:24
q Job 14:5
   Ps 139:16
   Ec 3:1,2
   Ec 8:7,8
   Mt 6:27
   Lu 12:25
r Lu 12:26
s 1Ch 29:25
   Mt 6:28,29
   Lu 12:27

the field today, and tomorrow is cast into a furnace — how much more *so* you, of little faith?[t]

40 "Do not store up for yourselves treasures on earth, where moth and rust destroy, and where thieves break in and steal —[u]

41 for where your treasure is, there your heart will be, too.[v]

42 "Therefore, do not be anxious, saying 'What might we eat?' or 'What might we drink?' or 'With what might we clothe ourselves?'[w]

43 "But search first for the kingdom of God, and all these things will be added to you.[y]

44 "Therefore, do not be anxious about tomorrow, for tomorrow will be anxious about itself.[y] Each day has enough trouble of its own.[z]

45 "For the kingdom of God is like a man, the master of a house, who went out early in the morning to hire workers for his vineyard.[a]

46 "And having agreed with the workmen on a denarius for the day, he sent them forth into his vineyard.[b]

47 "And having gone out about the [5]third hour, he

---
5 I.e., 9 a.m.

Notes:
t Mt 6:30; Lu 12:28
u Mt 6:19
v Mt 6:21; Lu 12:34
w Mt 6:31; Lu 12:29
x Mt 6:32; Lu 12:30
y Ps 37:4; Ps 127:2; Ps 145:15,16; Mt 6:33; Lu 12:31
y Pr 27:1
z Mt 6:34
a Mt 20:1
b Mt 20:2

The parable of the vineyard workers

saw others standing idle in the marketplace;[c]

48 and he said to them, 'Go also into the vineyard *to work*, and you will be paid whatever is just.'[d]

49 "And so they went. But again, having gone out about the [6]sixth and ninth hour, he did likewise.[e]

50 "But about the [7]eleventh *hour*, having gone out, he found others standing *there*, and said to them, 'Why are you standing here idle all day?'[f]

51 "They said to him, 'Because no one has hired us.' He said to them, 'You also, go into the vineyard, and whatever is right, you shall receive.'[g]

52 "But when the evening arrived, the master of the vineyard said to his foreman, 'Call the workmen and pay them their wages, beginning with the last until the first.'[h]

53 "And when those *hired* about the eleventh hour came, they each received a denarius.[i]

54 "And when those *hired* first came, they were thinking that they would receive more;[j] yet they *too* each received a denarius.[k]

55 "And having received *it*, they complained against

---

c Mt 20:3
d Mt 20:4
e Mt 20:5
f Mt 20:6
g Mt 20:7
h Mt 20:8
   Mt 20:16
i Mt 20:9
j Job 34:11
   Ps 62:12
   Jer 32:18,19
k Mt 20:10

---

6 I.e., noon and 3 p.m.
7 I.e., 5 p.m.

Jesus leads his followers forth to Jerusalem

^l *Mt 20:11*
^m *Ec 1:3*
   Ec 2:22
   Mt 20:12
ⁿ *Mt 20:13*
^o *Mt 5:45*
   Mt 20:14
^p *Mt 20:15*
   Mr 10:18
^q *Ps 78:52-54*
   Ps 107:10,14
^r *Mt 20:17*
   Mr 10:32
   Lu 18:31
^s *Mic 6:7*
^t *Mt 20:18,19*
   Mr 10:33
   Lu 18:32

the master of the house,[l]

56 saying, 'These *who came* last have worked one hour, and *yet* you have made them equal to us, the *ones* who have borne the burden of the day and the heat.'[m]

57 "But he answered to one of them, saying, 'Companion, I do not wrong you. Did you not agree with me *for* a denarius?[n]

58 "'Take what *is* yours and go. Yet I wish to give to this last *man*, even as *I have given* to you.[o]

59 "'Or is it not permitted for me to do as I wish with that which is mine? Or is your eye evil, because I am good?'"[p]

60 Now they were on the way, going up to Jerusalem, and Jesus was leading them forth,[q] and they were astonished; but those following were terrified. And once again, having taken the twelve, he began to tell them the things that were about to happen to him,[r]

61 because *he was saying*, "Behold, we are going up to Jerusalem, and the son of man will be handed over to the chief priests and to the scribes,[s] and they will condemn him to death.[t]

62 "And *they* will mock him and will spit upon him

and will flog him, and *they* will kill *him* and ⁸he will be raised up."ᵘ

u Mt 20:19
   Mr 10:34
   Lu 18:32,33

Chapter 11

AND having entered, he passed through Jericho.ᵃ

2 And behold, there was a man named Zacchaeus, and he was a chief tax collector, and he was rich.ᵇ

3 And he was seeking to see who Jesus was, and he was not able to from the crowd, because he was small in stature.ᶜ

4 And having run to the front, he climbed up onto a sycamore fig tree, that he might see him, for he was about to pass that *way*.ᵈ

5 And as he came to the place, having looked up, Jesus said to him, "Zacchaeus, hurry, come down! For today it behooves me to stay in your house."ᵉ

6 And having hurried, he came down and received him as a guest, rejoicing.ᶠ

a Mr 10:46
   Lu 19:1
b Lu 19:2
c Lu 19:3
d Lu 19:4
e Lu 19:5
f Lu 19:6

---

8 Certain later mss. add, *on the third day*

11 — The parable of the lost sheep

<small>
g Jer 16:8
  Lu 19:7
h Lu 15:3
i Mt 18:12
  Lu 15:4
j Mt 18:13
  Lu 15:5
k Lu 15:6
l Jer 12:7
  Mt 9:36
  Mt 15:24
  Mt 18:11
  Lu 19:10
m Mt 20:29
n Mr 10:46
o Mt 20:30
  Mr 10:47
  Lu 18:37,38
</small>

7 And having seen *it*, they all grumbled, saying, "He has gone in to find lodging with a sinful man."[g]

8 But he told them this parable, saying,[h]

9 "What man of you, having a hundred sheep, and having lost one of them, leaves not the ninety-nine in the wilderness, and goes after that *one* which has been lost, until he finds it?[i]

10 "And having found it, he lays it on his shoulders, rejoicing.[j]

11 "And having come to the house, he calls together *his* friends and neighbors, saying to them, 'Rejoice with me, for I have found my sheep, the *one that* was lost!'[k]

12 "For the son of man has come to search for and save that which has been lost."[l]

13 And as he was going out from Jericho, and his disciples and a large crowd,[m] *the* son of Timaeus, Bartimaeus, a blind beggar, was seated beside the road.[n]

14 And having heard that it was Jesus of Nazareth, he began to cry out and to say, "Jesus, son of David, have mercy on me!"[o]

15 And many rebuked him, that he should keep

The blind beggar recovers his sight 11

silent; but he cried out much more, *saying,* "Son of David, have mercy on me!"[p]

16 And having stopped, Jesus said, "Summon him." And they called the blind *man,* saying to him, "Take heart, rise up — he calls you!"[q]

17 And having thrown aside his cloak, *and* having risen up, he came to Jesus.[r]

18 And answering him, Jesus said, "What do you wish, that I should do to you?" But the blind man said to him, "Rabboni, that I might recover *my* sight."[s]

19 And Jesus said to him, "Go your way, your faith has healed you." And immediately, he recovered sight, and he followed him on the way.[t]

20 And when they approached Jerusalem and came to Bethphage, on the mount of Olives, then Jesus sent two disciples,[u]

21 saying to them, "Go into the village that is opposite you, and immediately, entering into it, you will find ¹a donkey tied *there*; and having untied *it*, bring it.[v]

22 "And if anyone says anything to you, you will

---

p Mt 20:31
   Mr 10:48
   Lu 18:39
q Mr 10:49
   Lu 18:40
r Mr 10:50
s Mt 20:32,33
   Mr 10:51
   Lu 18:41
t Mt 20:34
   Mr 10:52
   Lu 18:42,43
u Mt 21:1
   Mr 11:1
   Lu 19:29
v Mt 21:2
   Mr 11:2
   Lu 19:30

---

1 According to the best ancient mss.; certain later mss. read, *a young ass*; one late ms. reads, *a colt*

11   Jesus enters Jerusalem on a donkey   The fig tree

<small>
w   Mt 21:3
     Mr 11:3
     Lu 19:31
x   Mt 21:6
     Mr 11:4-6
     Lu 19:32-34
y   Ge 22:2,3
     Zec 9:9
     Mt 21:7
     Mr 11:7
     Lu 19:35
     Jn 12:14
z   Mt 21:17
     Mr 11:11
a   Mt 21:18
     Mr 11:12
b   Mt 21:19
     Mr 11:13
c   Jer 8:13
d   Mt 21:19
     Mr 11:14
</small>

say, 'The teacher has need of it', and immediately he will send it back here.'"ʷ

23 And the disciples, having gone, and having done as Jesus had arranged with them,ˣ

24 brought the donkey, and they placed their cloaks upon *its back*, and he sat on them.ʸ

25 And he entered into Jerusalem, into the temple. And having looked all around on all things *there*, the hour being now late, he went out to Bethany, with the twelve.ᶻ

26 And the following day, when they had gone out from Bethany, he was hungry.ᵃ

27 And having seen from a distance a fig tree having leaves, he went *to see* therefore if he will find any *fruit* on it; and having come to it, he found nothing except leaves, for it was not the season for figs.ᵇ

28 And he answered, saying to it, "No longer in this age, may *there be* from you *even* one fruit to eat."ᶜ And his disciples heard *this*.ᵈ

29 And they came to Jerusalem, and having entered into the temple, he began to drive out those selling and those buying in the temple, and he overturned the tables of the moneychangers and the seats of those

selling the doves.^e

30 And he was teaching and was saying to them, "Has it not been written, MY HOUSE WILL BE CALLED A HOUSE OF PRAYER FOR ALL THE NATIONS.^f But you have made it A DEN OF ROBBERS."^g

31 And the chief priests and scribes heard of *it*, for all the crowd was thunderstruck by his teaching.^h

32 And whenever evening came, he went forth out of the city.^i

33 And passing by early in the morning, they saw the fig tree, withered from the roots *up*.^j

34 And having remembered, Simon said to him, "Rabbi, look, the fig tree which you cursed is withered!"^k

35 And answering, Jesus said to them, "Have *the* faith of God.^l

36 "Truly I say to you, whoever might say to this mountain,^m 'Be you raised up and be cast into the sea',^n and might not waver in his heart, but might believe that what he says takes place, it will be *thus* for him.^o

37 "On account of this, I say to you, all *things* whatsoever – and praying^p – *for which* you ask, keep believing that you have received *them*, and it will be

e Mt 21:12
   Mr 11:15
f Isa 56:7
g Jer 7:11
   Mt 21:13
   Mr 11:17
   Lu 19:46
h Mr 11:18
i Mr 11:19
   Lu 21:37
j Mr 11:20
k Joe 1:12,15,19
   Mr 11:21
l Eze 28:16
   Mr 11:22
m Ps 48:1
   Ps 125:1
   Isa 56:7
   Eze 20:40
   Joe 3:17
   Zec 8:3
n Re 8:8
o Jer 51:25,26
   Mt 21:21
   Mr 11:23
p Mt 26:39
   Mr 14:35,36
   Lu 22:41,42

11   The chief priests question Jesus

so for you."[q]

38 And it came to pass on one of the days, as he was teaching the people in the temple,[r] that the chief priests were present, and the scribes with the elders.[s]

39 And they spoke, saying to him, "Tell us by what authority you are doing these things, or who is the *one* who gave this authority to you?"[t]

40 But answering, he said to them, "I also will request *of* you a statement, and you tell me —[u]

41 the baptism of John, was it from heaven or from men?"[v]

42 And they reasoned among themselves, saying, "If we say, 'From heaven', he will say, 'So then, why did you not believe him?'[w]

43 "But if we say, 'From men', all the people will stone us, for they are persuaded *that* John was a prophet."[x]

44 And having answered Jesus, they said, "We do not know." And Jesus said to them, "Neither *then will* I tell you by what authority I do these things."[y]

45 But he began to say this parable to the people:[z] "A certain well-born man went to a distant region to take a kingdom for himself and to return.[a]

---

q   Mt 21:22
    Mr 11:24
r   Lu 21:38
s   Mt 21:23
    Mr 11:27
    Lu 20:1
t   Isa 40:14
    Mt 21:23
    Mr 11:28
    Lu 20:2
u   Mt 21:24
    Mr 11:29
    Lu 20:3
v   Mt 21:25
    Mr 11:30
    Lu 20:4
w   Mt 21:25
    Mr 11:31
    Lu 20:5
x   De 18:15,18
    Mt 21:26
    Mr 11:32
    Lu 20:6
y   Mt 21:27
    Mr 11:33
    Lu 20:7,8
z   Lu 20:9
a   Isa 45:23
    Lu 19:12

The parable of the minas

46 "Now having summoned ten of his slaves,[b] he gave to them ten [2]minas,[c] and said to them, 'Do business *with this* until I return.'[d]

47 "But his citizens hated him,[e] and they sent an emissary[f] after him, saying, 'We do not wish this *man* to reign over us.'[g]

48 "And it came to pass upon his return *from* having taken the kingdom, that he called the slaves to whom he gave the money to be summoned, so that he might know what each had gained by trading.[h]

49 "Now the first *one* came, saying, 'Master, your mina has gained ten minas *more*.'[i]

50 "And he said to him, 'Well done, good slave. Since you were faithful with very little, be you having authority over ten cities.'[j]

51 "And the second *one* came, saying, 'Your mina, Master, has made five minas *more*.'[k]

52 "And he said to this *one* also, 'And you, be over five cities.'[l]

53 "And another *one* came, saying, 'Master, I knew that you are a harsh man,[m] reaping where you did not

---

b Le 25:55
  Nu 18:21
  Isa 44:21
c Eze 45:12
d Mt 21:45
  Mt 25:14
  Lu 19:13
e De 9:24
  Ne 9:26
  Ps 50:17
  Isa 1:2
  Isa 30:9
f Mt 20:28
  Mr 10:45
g 1Sa 8:7
  Ps 78:56
  Pr 29:2
  Jer 2:29-31
  Jer 5:3-5,23
  Lu 19:14
h Mt 25:19
  Lu 19:15
i Mt 25:20
  Lu 19:16
j Nu 35:2-7
  Jos 21:1-42
  Mt 25:21
  Lu 19:17
k Mt 25:22
  Lu 19:18
l Mt 25:23
  Lu 19:19
m De 29:20
  Jos 24:19,20
  Isa 27:11
  Jer 13:14
  Jer 16:3,4
  Eze 7:9
  Eze 8:18

---

2 An ancient Near Eastern measure of weight, one mina was equivalent to 100 drachmæ, or about 88 denarii

The parable of the minas

sow,ⁿ and gathering together from where you did not scatter.ᵒ

54 "'And having been terrified, *you* having gone away,ᵖ I hid your mina in the ground; see then, *you* have what *is* yours.'ᑫ

55 "He said to him, 'Out of your own mouth will I judge you, wicked slave! You knew that I am a harsh man,ʳ reaping where I have not sowed, and gathering together from where I have not scattered.ˢ

56 "'And on account of this, why did you not give my money to the ³bank; and having come, I might have collected it with interest?'ᵗ

57 "And to those standing there, he said, 'Take the mina away from him, and give *it to* the *one who* has the ten minas.ᵘ

58 "'Moreover, these enemies of mineᵛ — the *ones who* have not been willing for me to reign over them — bring them here and slay them before me.'ʷ

59 And having heard his parables, the chief priests realized that he was speaking about them.ˣ

---

n Ex 23:16,19
   Le 27:30
   De 26:10
   Jn 4:37
o Ex 13:2,12
   Ex 22:29,30
   Mt 25:24
   Lu 19:21
p Ps 42:3,9,10
   Ps 71:10,11
   Ps 115:2
   Isa 49:14
   Jer 12:7
   La 5:20
q Mt 25:25
   Lu 19:20
r Pr 28:15
   Ho 13:7,8
s Mal 3:8
   Mt 25:26
   Lu 19:22
t Ex 22:25
   De 23:19
   Ps 15:2,5
   Pr 28:16
   Jer 17:11
   Jer 22:17
   Mt 25:27
   Lu 19:23
u Mt 25:28
   Lu 19:24
v Ps 74:23
w De 7:10
   De 32:41
   Ps 21:8
   Isa 59:18
   Isa 65:2,12,15
   Isa 66:6
   Jer 11:3,4,8,11
   La 3:42,43
   Lu 19:27
x Mt 21:45

---

3 Lit., *table*; i.e., a money-changer's stall

Is it lawful to pay tribute to Caesar?

CHAPTER 12

AND having watched him closely, they sent spies, feigning themselves to be righteous, that they might take hold of him *for some* statement, so as to hand him over to the governor's rule and authority.[a]

2 And they questioned him, saying, "Teacher, we know that you speak and teach rightly, and do not take sides, but teach the way of God on the basis of truth.[b]

3 "Is it lawful for us to give tribute[c] to Caesar, or not? Should we give, or not give?"[d]

4 But having perceived their craftiness,[e] he said to them,[f]

5 "Show me a ¹denarius. Whose likeness and inscription does it have?" And they said, "Caesar's."[g]

6 But he said to them, "Well then, give back the

a Mt 22:15,16
   Mr 12:13
   Lu 20:20
b Mt 22:16
   Mr 12:14
   Lu 20:21
c Ezr 7:24
   Ps 89:22
d Jer 27:1-8
   Jer 27:11-15
   Mt 22:17
   Mr 12:14
   Lu 20:22
e Mt 22:18
   Mr 12:15
f Lu 20:23
g Mt 22:19-21
   Mr 12:16
   Lu 20:24

---

1 A Roman coin, originally of silver; at that time, the denarius bore the portrait of Tiberius Caesar, whose reign lasted from 14–37 CE

things of Caesar to Caesar, and the *things* of God to God."ʰ

7   And they were not able to take hold of him in his discourse in the presence of the people; and having marveled at his answer, they were silent.ⁱ

8   But having come near, some of the Sadducees, who contend that there is no resurrection, questioned him,ʲ

9   saying, "Teacher, Moses wrote to us, IF ANYONE'S BROTHER SHOULD DIE, having a wife, AND HE IS CHILDLESS, THAT HIS BROTHER SHOULD TAKE THE WIFE, AND SHOULD RAISE UP OFFSPRING TO HIS BROTHER.ᵏ

10   "Now then, there were seven brothers, and the first, having taken a wife, died childless.ˡ

11   "And the second *took her as* wife, and he died childless.ᵐ

12   "And the third took her, and also in like manner the seven, *and they* did not leave behind children, and died.ⁿ

13   "And afterwards, the woman died.ᵒ

14   "Therefore, the wife, in the resurrection, whenever they rise up, *the* wife of which of them does

---

h Ex 30:13
   Mt 17:24,25
   Mt 22:21
   Mr 12:17
   Lu 20:25
i Mt 22:22
   Mr 12:17
   Lu 20:26
j Mt 22:23
   Mr 12:18
   Lu 20:27
k De 25:5,6
   Mt 22:24
   Mr 12:19
   Lu 20:28
l Mt 22:25
   Mr 12:20
   Lu 20:29
m Mt 22:26
   Mr 12:21
   Lu 20:30
n Mt 22:26
   Mr 12:21,22
   Lu 20:31
o Mt 22:27
   Mr 12:22
   Lu 20:32

she become? For the seven had her as wife."ᵖ

15 And Jesus said to them, "The sons of this age marry and are given in marriage.ᑫ

16 "But those having been deemed worthy to hit upon that age and the resurrection – the *resurrection out from among the dead* – neither marry nor are given in marriage.ʳ

17 "For neither are they still able to die, for they are equal to angels, and are sons of God,ˢ being sons of the resurrection.ᵗ

18 "But that the dead are raised up, Moses also showed at the bush, when the LORD called *Himself* THE GOD OF ABRAHAM, AND GOD OF ISAAC, AND GOD OF JACOB.ᵘ

19 "Now He is not the God of the dead, but of the living, for *they* all live *with* Him."ᵛ

20 But having answered, some of the scribes said *to him*, "Teacher, you have spoken well."ʷ

21 Therefore the Jews were marveling, saying, "How does this man know written works, not having studied?"ˣ

22 ²But having drawn him aside privately, away

---
2 Most later mss. omit verses 22-26

p *Mt* 22:28
   Mr 12:23
   Lu 20:33
q *Lu* 20:34
r *Mt* 22:30
   Mr 12:25
   Lu 20:35
s *Ge* 28:12,13
   Gob 1:6
t *Mt* 22:30
   Mr 12:25
   Lu 20:36
u *Ex* 3:6,15
   Mt 22:31,32
   Mr 12:26
   Lu 20:37
v *Ps* 78:23-25
   Ps 148:2
   Mt 22:32
   Mr 12:27
   Lu 20:38
w *Lu* 20:39
x *Jn* 7:15

The foremost commandment

from the crowd, some of his disciples questioned him about this, saying, "When will this be, *that* the dead are raised up?"[y]

23 But having answered, he said *to them*, "Do not be misled, for HE WHO GOES DOWN TO SHEOL SHALL NOT COME UP,[z]

24 NOR SHALL HE RETURN[a] FROM THE LAND OF DARKNESS AND DEEP SHADOW.[b]

25 "For the man who dies is not wakened from sleep, nor *is he* raised up;[c]

26 but all go to the same place,[d] and the spirit will return to God who gave *it*."[e]

27 And having come near, one of the [3]councilors — having heard them discussing *the matter* together *and* having seen that he answered them well — questioned him, "Which is the foremost commandment?"[f]

28 Jesus answered, "The foremost is, HEAR, O ISRAEL! THE LORD OUR GOD IS ONE;[g]

29 AND YOU WILL LOVE THE LORD YOUR GOD WITH ALL YOUR HEART, AND WITH ALL YOUR SOUL, AND WITH ALL YOUR MIND, AND WITH ALL YOUR

---

[y] Ps 30:3
Ps 44:25,26
Isa 26:19
Eze 37:4-6
Eze 37:12-14
Da 12:2
[z] Job 7:9
Ps 89:48
[a] 2Sa 12:23
Job 16:22
Ps 78:39
Ps 103:15,16
[b] Job 10:21,22
[c] Job 14:10-12
Ps 89:48
Isa 26:14
[d] Ge 3:19
Ps 104:29
Ec 3:19,20
Ec 9:2-10
[e] Ge 1:2
Ge 2:7
Ps 104:30
Ec 12:7
Isa 42:5
[f] Mt 22:35,36
Mr 12:28
[g] De 6:4
Mr 12:29

---

3 According to the best ancient mss.; subsequent mss. read, *scribes*; certain late mss. read, *lawyers*

STRENGTH.[h]

30 "This is the great and first commandment.[i]

31 "But a second is like it: YOU WILL LOVE YOUR NEIGHBOR AS YOURSELF.[j] There is not another commandment greater than these."[k]

32 And the [4]councilor said to him, "Right, Teacher, in accordance with truth have you said that HE IS ONE,[l] and THERE IS NO OTHER BESIDES HIM;[m]

33 and to LOVE HIM WITH ALL THE HEART, AND WITH ALL THE UNDERSTANDING, AND WITH ALL THE SOUL, AND WITH ALL THE STRENGTH,[n] and to LOVE ONE'S NEIGHBOR AS ONESELF,[o] is greater than all the burnt offerings and sacrifices."[p]

34 And Jesus, having seen that he answered wisely, said to him, "You are not far from the kingdom of God."[q] And none dared to question him any longer.[r]

35 Then *some* from the crowd, having heard these words, said, "This is truly the prophet."[s]

36 Others said, "This is the [5]messiah."[t] But the *others* said, "Surely not — for does the [5]messiah come out of Galilee?[u]

---

4 According to the best ancient mss.; subsequent mss. read, *scribe*; certain late mss. read, *lawyer*
5 Gr., *messias*, for the Hebrew *mashiach*; certain later mss. read, *christos*

[h] De 6:5
   Mt 22:37
   Mr 12:30
[i] Mt 22:38
[j] Le 19:18,33,34
   Le 25:23,55
   De 14:1
   1Ch 29:15
[k] Mt 22:39,40
   Mr 12:31
[l] De 6:4
[m] De 4:39
   Mr 12:32
[n] De 6:5
[o] Le 19:18
[p] Ex 13:2,12-15
   Ex 29:36-42
   Le 1:1-17
   Le 2:1-16
   Le 3:1-17
   Le 4:1-35
   Le 5:1-19
   Le 6:1-23
   Le 7:1-5
   Le 14:1-32
   Le 16:3-34
   Le 17:1-6
   Le 23:1-38
   Le 24:5-8
   Nu 28:1-31
   Nu 29:1-40
   2Ch 8:12,13
   Ezr 3:1-5
   Jer 33:18
   Eze 43:18-27
   Eze 45:13-25
   Eze 46:1-15
   Mal 1:11
   Mr 12:33
[q] Ge 1:2
   Mr 15:43
   Jn 3:5
   Jn 4:24
[r] Mt 22:46
   Mr 12:34
   Lu 20:40
[s] Mt 21:11
   Jn 7:40
[t] Jn 7:31
[u] Jn 7:41

Is the messiah David's son?   Beware of the scribes

37 "Has not the Scripture said that the ⁶messiah comes out from the offspring of David,ᵛ and from Bethlehem, the village where David was?"ʷ

38 Then a dissension came about in the crowd on account of him.ˣ

39 But he said to them, "Wherefore do they say *that* the ⁶messiah is the son of David?ʸ

40 "For David himself says in the book of Psalms,

> 'THE LORD SAID TO MY LORD,
> "SIT AT MY RIGHT HAND,
> UNTIL I MIGHT MAKE OF YOUR ENEMIES
> A FOOTSTOOL FOR YOUR FEET."' ᶻ

41 "So *if* David calls him LORD, then wherefore is he his son?" And the great crowd enjoyed listening to him.ᵃ

42 But *as* all the people were listening *to him*, he said to his disciples,ᵇ

43 "Beware of the scribes, who like to walk in long robes, and are fond of greetings in the marketplaces, and chief seats in the synagogues, and places of honor at the banquets;ᶜ

44 who wolf down the households of widows,ᵈ and

---

6 Gr., *messias*, for the Hebrew *mashiach*; certain later mss. read, *christos*

---

v 2Sa 7:5-16
   Ps 89:3,4
   Ps 89:20,26-29
   Ps 89:35,36
   Eze 34:23,24
   Eze 37:24,25
w 1Sa 17:12,15,58
   Mic 5:2
   Jn 7:42
x Jn 7:43
y Mt 22:42
   Mr 12:35
   Lu 20:41
   Lu 23:2
z Ps 110:1
   Mt 22:44
   Mr 12:36
   Lu 20:42,43
a Mt 22:45
   Mr 12:37
   Lu 20:44
b Mt 23:1
   Lu 20:45
c Mt 23:6,7
   Mr 12:38,39
   Lu 20:46
d Isa 3:14,15
   Isa 10:1,2

The chief priests and the Pharisees seek to arrest Jesus

pray at length to shine before *others*. These will receive judgment exceedingly."[e]

45 And there was much muttering about him among the crowds, for some said, "He is good"; but others said, "But no – he leads the people astray!"[f]

46 The Pharisees heard the crowd murmuring these things about him, and the chief priests and the Pharisees sent attendants, that they might lay hold of him.[g]

47 Now some of them were willing to lay hold of him, but no one laid hands on him.[h]

48 The attendants therefore came to the chief priests and the Pharisees, and they said to them, "Why did you not bring him?"[i]

49 The attendants answered, "No man ever spoke like this."[j]

50 Then the Pharisees answered, "Have you not also been led astray?[k]

51 "No one of the rulers has believed in him, nor of the Pharisees.[l]

52 "But this crowd, which does not know the Law, is accursed."[m]

53 Nicodemus said to them, "Our Law does not

e Mr 12:40
  Lu 20:47
f Jn 7:12
  Jn 10:20
g Jn 7:32
h Jn 7:44
i Jn 7:45
j Jn 7:46
k Jn 7:47
l Jn 7:48
m Jn 7:49

judge the man, before it might hear from him first, and might know what he does."ⁿ

54 And they answered, saying to him, "Are you not also from Galilee? Search and see, because a prophet out of Galilee does not arise."ᵒ

n *Jn 7:50,51*
o *Jn 7:52*

Chapter 13

AND having sat down opposite the treasury, he contemplated how the crowd cast money into the treasury; and many rich people were casting *in* much.ᵃ

2 And he saw a certain poor widow casting *in* two ¹small coins;ᵇ

3 and he said, "Truly I say to you, that this poor widow has cast *in* more than all.ᶜ

4 "For these all cast *in* gifts from out of their abundance — but she, from out of her penury, did cast *in* all *that* she had to live on."ᵈ

5 And as he was going forth out from the temple,

a *Mr 12:41*
   Lu 21:1
b *De 15:4*
   Mr 12:42
   Lu 21:2
c *Mr 12:43*
   Lu 21:3
d *Job 30:25*
   Mr 12:44
   Lu 21:4

---

1 Gr., *lepta*; the *leptos* was a small copper or bronze coin

The tribulations to come

one of his disciples said to him, "Teacher, behold — such stones, and such buildings!"[e]

6 And Jesus said to him, "Do you see these great buildings? Not a stone upon stone shall be left here, which shall not be thrown down."[f]

7 And they questioned him, saying, "Teacher, how long therefore *until* these things, and what will be the sign when these things are about to happen?"[g]

8 But he said, "Take heed, lest you be led astray. For many will come in my name, saying 'I AM',[2][h] and they will lead many astray.[i]

9 "But when you might hear *of* battles and rumors of battles, do not be unsettled, for this must come to pass. However, it is not yet the end.[j]

10 "For nation will rise up against nation, and kingdom against kingdom;[k] there will be earthquakes in places *everywhere*;[l] there will be famines.[m]

11 "And a brother will hand over a brother to death, and a father *his* child, and children will rise up against parents, and will put them to death.[n]

12 "And you will be hated by all on account of my name, but the *one* having remained behind to the end,

---

2 Certain later mss. add, *the Christ*

---

e Ezr 1:2-4
Ezr 6:3-16
Mt 24:1
Mr 13:1
Lu 21:5

f 1Ki 9:6-9
Jer 51:25,26
Mt 24:2
Mr 13:2
Lu 21:6

g Isa 26:21
Mt 24:3
Mr 13:4
Lu 21:7

h Ex 3:14
Ex 6:2,3
Ex 20:7

i Mt 24:4,5
Mr 13:5,6
Lu 21:8

j Eze 7:2-4
Mt 24:6
Mr 13:7
Lu 21:9

k De 28:48,49
2Ch 15:6
Jer 5:15
Joe 3:9,11,12
Am 6:14

l Jer 49:21
Joe 2:1,10
Am 8:8

k De 28:53
Eze 5:16,17
Eze 7:15

m Mt 24:7
Mr 13:8
Lu 21:10,11

n Ex 32:25-29
De 28:54,56
Isa 9:19
Mic 7:2,6
Mr 13:12

The Gospel of Jesus of Nazareth

13   "If anyone says, 'Behold, the messiah!', do not believe it"

he will be saved.⁰

13 "But when you might see Jerusalem being encircled by ³armies, then know that her desolation has drawn near.ᵖ

14 "Then let those in Judea flee to the mountains,ᑫ and let those in the midst of her depart, and do not let those in the countryside enter into her;ʳ

15 because these are days of vengeance,ˢ and judgment,ᵗ that all things which have been written may be fulfilled.ᵘ

16 "But the *one* upon the housetop, let him not come down, nor go in to take anything out of his house;ᵛ

17 and the *one* in the field, let him not turn back to the things behind, to pick up his clothing.ʷ

18 "But woe to those who are pregnant, and to those who are nursing in those days;ˣ

19 for there will be great distress upon the land, and wrath *upon* this people.ʸ

20 "And then, if anyone says to you, 'Behold, here is the ⁴messiah! Behold, there!', do not believe it.ᶻ

---

3 Or, *hosts*; certain later mss. read, *encamped armies*
4 Gr., *messias*, for the Hebrew *mashiach*; certain later mss. read, *christos*

Margin references:
o   Mt 24:13; Mr 13:13; Lu 17:23; Lu 21:17,19
p   Jer 9:11; Jer 19:8; Joe 1:15; Joe 2:1-11; Lu 21:20
q   Ge 19:17; Mt 24:16; Mr 13:14
r   Lu 21:21
s   De 32:35,41; Pr 6:34; Na 1:2,6
t   Eze 5:8,15; Eze 11:10; Eze 14:21; Eze 16:38
u   Mt 5:17; Lu 18:31; Lu 21:22
v   Mt 24:17; Mr 13:15; Lu 17:31
w   Mt 24:18; Mr 13:16; Lu 17:31
x   Mt 24:19; Mr 13:17
y   Isa 10:23; Isa 13:9,15,16; Jer 11:11; Eze 7:2-27; Eze 21:31,32; Eze 33:20,27-29; Lu 21:23
z   Mr 13:21; Mr 16:9-13; Mr 16:14; Lu 24:32-35; Jn 20:18,24,25; Jn 20:30,31; Jn 21:1,14; Act 1:3; Act 17:2,3
a   Mr 13:22; Act 2:38-43; Act 5:12-16; Act 6:7,8

21 "For false *messiahs* and false prophets will rise up, and will give signs and wonders, and lead many astray.[a]

22 "But you, take heed, *for* I have told you all things in advance.[b]

23 "But in those days, after that tribulation, THE SUN WILL BE DARKENED, AND THE MOON WILL NOT GIVE ITS LIGHT,[c]

24 AND THE STARS WILL FALL FROM HEAVEN, AND THE POWERS OF THE HEAVENS WILL BE SHAKEN.[d]

25 "But *when* these things are beginning to happen, then straighten yourselves and lift up your heads,[e] because your redemption draws near."[f]

26 And he told them a parable, *saying*, "Behold the fig tree, and all of the trees — already when they put forth buds, looking, you yourselves realize that the summer is already near.[g]

27 "And so, when you see these things coming to pass, realize that He[h] is near, at the doors.[i]

28 "Truly I say to you, that this generation shall not pass away, until all these things shall have happened.[j]

29 "Heaven and earth will pass away, but in no wise will my words pass away.[k]

a Act 8:6,7,13
   Act 9:32-42
   Act 14:1,3,8-10
   Act 19:1-8,11,12
   2Co 12:12
b Mt 16:16,20
   Mr 13:23
   1Jn 2:4
c Isa 13:10
   Eze 32:7,8
   Joe 2:10,30,31
   Joe 3:14,15
   Am 5:18,20
   Mt 24:29
   Mr 13:24
d Isa 13:13
   Hag 2:6,21
   Mt 24:29
   Mr 13:25
   Lu 21:25,26
e De 7:10
   Ps 83:2
   Isa 63:10
   La 2:4,5
f Ps 106:10
   Mt 20:28
   Mr 10:45
   Lu 21:28
   Jn 8:33
   Jn 8:35,36
g Mt 24:32
   Mr 13:28
   Lu 21:29,30
h Nu 16:20,21,33
   Lu 12:5
   Jn 14:30
i 1Ki 6:31,32
   Eze 43:4-9
   Mt 24:33
   Mr 13:29
   Lu 21:31
j Jer 16:9
   Eze 12:25,28
   Mt 24:34
   Mr 13:30
   Lu 21:32
k Mt 5:18
   Mt 24:35
   Mr 13:31
   Lu 21:33

"Be vigilant!"

30 "But with regard to that day and hour, no one knows.[l]

31 [5]["But attend to yourselves, lest when your hearts be burdened with hangover and drunkenness, that day should come upon you suddenly —[m]

32 for like a snare it will come upon all those sitting upon the face of the earth.[n]]

33 "Look! Be awake! For you do not know on what sort of day your master comes.[o]

34 "*It is* like a man who went away from his people,[p] and leaving his house, he charged his slaves[q] with authority, to each one his work, and commanded his doorkeepers[r] to be vigilant.[s]

35 "Therefore, be vigilant! For you do not know when the master of the house[t] is coming[u] — whether in the evening, or at midnight, or at cockcrow, or in the morning —[v]

36 lest, having come suddenly, he might find you sleeping.[w]

37 "But what I say to you, I say to all: be vigilant!"[x]

38 Now the feast of Unleavened *Bread*[y] was approaching.[z]

---

l Mt 24:35
  Mr 13:31
m Lu 21:34
n Isa 24:17
  Zep 1:2,3,18
  Lu 21:35
o Mt 24:42
  Mr 13:33
p Ps 13:1
  Ps 22:2
  Ps 42:3
  Ps 71:10,11
  Ps 115:2
  Isa 49:14
  Jer 12:7
q Le 25:55
  Isa 44:21
r Ge 3:24
  Ex 25:18-20
  Eze 10:19
s Mr 13:34
t 2Ch 2:4,5
  2Ch 7:1,2
  Eze 43:4,5
u Jn 14:30
v Mr 13:35
w Mr 13:36
x Mr 13:37
y Ex 12:1-20,24
  Le 23:5-7
  Nu 9:2,3
  De 16:1,12
z Lu 22:1

5 Verses 31 and 32 are not found in the best ancient mss.

Caiaphas — The costly spikenard — 13

39 Then the chief priests and the scribes and the elders of the people were gathered together in the court of the high priest, who was called ⁶Caiaphas.[a]

40 And they were seeking how to lay hold of him;[b]

41 but they were saying, "Not during the feast, so that there not be an uproar among the people."[c]

42 And as he was in Bethany, in the house of Simon the leper, he reclined at his table, *and there* came a woman who had an alabaster *phial* of very costly pure spikenard ointment; and having broken the alabaster *phial's seal*, she poured *it* on his head.[d]

43 But having seen *this*, the disciples became indignant, saying, "What is the point of this waste?"[e]

44 "For this could have been sold for much, and *the proceeds* given to the poor!"[f] And they admonished her sternly.[g]

45 But Jesus, having realized *this*, said to them, "Leave her alone. Why do you give her trouble? For she did a good deed to me.[h]

46 "For the poor you have with you always,[i] and whenever you wish, you are always able to do good

---

a Mt 26:3
b Mt 26:4
   Mr 14:1
c Mt 26:5
   Mr 14:2
d Ca 1:12,13
   Mt 26:6,7
   Mr 14:3
e Mt 26:8
   Mr 14:4
f De 15:4-6,10
   Pr 19:17
   Pr 28:27
   Mt 26:9
   Jn 12:5
g Mr 14:5
h Mt 26:10
   Mr 14:6
i De 15:11

---

6 Joseph Caiaphas, a high priest of the Jews from 18 – 36 CE and presumably presider, or *Nasi*, of the Great Sanhedrin at the trial of Jesus

13,14   *Judas meets with the chief priests*

<small>
j   Mt 26:11
    Mr 14:7
    Jn 12:8
k   Mt 26:12
    Mr 14:8
l   Mt 26:14
    Mr 14:10
    Jn 18:15
m   Ex 12:3
    Zec 11:12
    Mt 26:15
    Mr 14:11
    Lu 22:4,5
n   Mt 26:16
    Mr 14:11
    Lu 22:6
</small>

to them; but you do not always have me.[j]

47 "For this woman, having poured this ointment on my body, has anointed my body for burial."[k]

48 Then one of the twelve,[7] having gone to the chief priests,[l]

49 was saying, "What are you willing to give me? And I will hand him over to you." And they reckoned to him thirty silver coins.[m]

50 And he agreed, and was seeking a fitting time to hand him over to them, apart from the crowd.[n]

Chapter 14

<small>
a   De 16:3
b   Ho 6:2,3
    Ho 6:6
    Mt 26:2
    Mr 14:1
c   Mr 14:13
d   Ex 12:19
    Ex 13:7
    Lu 22:8
</small>

NOW it was to be the Passover and the unleavened *loaves*[a] after two days.[b]

2 And he sent two of his disciples,[c] having said *to them*, "Having gone, make ready the Passover for us, that we might eat *it*."[d]

3 But they said to him, "Where do you wish *that*

<small>7 Certain later mss. add, *who is called Judas Iscariot*</small>

The Last Supper 14

we should prepare *for it*?"[e]

4 And he said to them, "Behold, *upon* you having gone into the city, a man carrying a pitcher of water will meet you. Follow him into the house that he enters.[f]

5 "And you will say to the master of the house, 'The teacher says to you, "Where is the lodge, where I might eat the Passover with my disciples?"'[g]

6 "And he will show you a large upper room *that is* furnished. Prepare *for it* there."[h]

7 And having gone away from *there*, they found *it* just as he had said it to them, and they prepared *for* the Passover.[i]

8 But evening having come, he reclined *at table* with the twelve.[j]

9 And he said to them, "With passionate yearning, I longed to eat this Passover with you, before I suffer.[k]

10 "For I say to you, that I will never eat it, until it be fulfilled[l] in the kingdom of God."[m]

11 And he rose from the supper, and laying aside the outer garments, and having taken a towel, he girded himself.[n]

12 Then he poured water into the basin, and he

e Mt 26:17
   Mr 14:12
   Lu 22:9
f Mr 14:13
   Lu 22:10
g Mt 26:18
   Mr 14:14
   Lu 22:11
h Mr 14:15
i Mt 26:19
   Mr 14:16
   Lu 22:13
j Mt 26:20
   Mr 14:17
   Lu 22:14
k Ps 22:14-18
   Isa 53:4-6,10
   Lu 22:15
   Heb 10:30,31
l Ex 6:6
   Ex 12:26,27,42
   Ex 13:3
m Lu 22:16
n Jn 13:4

Jesus washes his disciples' feet

began to wash the disciples' feet, and to wipe *them* with the towel with which he was girded.º

13 Then he came to Simon, who said to him, "Master, do you wash my feet?"ᵖ

14 And Jesus answered him, saying, "What I do, you do not see just now, but you will come to know after these *examples*."ᑫ

15 And Simon said to him, "Never should you wash my feet, ¹*not* ever!" Jesus answered him, "If I do not wash you, you have no part with me."ʳ

16 Simon said to him, "Master, not only my feet, but also *my* hands and *my* head!"ˢ

17 Jesus said to him, "The one who has bathed has no *other* need except to wash the feet; otherwise, he is completely clean. And you are clean, but not all *of you*."ᵗ

18 Therefore, when he had washed their feet, and taken his outer garments, and having reclined again at table, he said to them, "Do you realize what I have done to you?"ᵘ

19 "You call me 'the teacher' and 'the master', and you say *so* correctly, for *I* am."ᵛ

---

o *Jn 13:5*
p *Jn 13:6*
q Lu 7:38,44-46
    Jn 13:7
r Isa 52:2
    Jn 13:8
s *Jn 13:9*
t *Jn 13:10*
u *Jn 13:12*
v *Jn 13:13*

---

1 Lit., *to the age*

20 "Therefore, if I, the 'master' and the 'teacher', have washed your feet, *then* you also ought to wash one another's feet."[w]

21 "For I have given you an example, so that just as I have done to you, you also should do."[x]

22 "Truly, truly, I say to you, [2]a teacher is not above the disciple, nor *is* a master above his slave."[y]

23 "If you know these things, you are blessed if you do them."[z]

24 And *as* they were eating of them, having taken bread, and having blessed *it*, he broke *it*, and gave *it* to them, and said, "Take, eat — this is my body."[a]

25 And having taken a cup, *and* having given thanks, he gave *it* to them, and they all drank of it.[b]

26 And he said to them, "This is my blood[c] of the covenant, which is being poured out for many.[d]

27 "Truly I say to you, that I will never again drink of the fruit of the vine, until that day when I might drink it fresh in the kingdom of God.[e]

28 "I give to you a fresh commandment,[f] that *you* love one another — just as I have loved you, so that you

---

w Jn 13:14
x Jn 13:15
y Mt 10:24
Jn 13:16
z Jn 13:17
a Le 3:17
Le 7:25
Mt 26:26
Mr 14:22
Lu 22:19
Jn 6:55,56
b Le 3:17
Le 7:27
Mt 26:27
Mr 14:23
Lu 22:17
Jn 6:55,56
c Le 17:10,11,14
d Ex 24:4-8
De 12:16
Ps 49:7,8
Isa 53:10,11
Zec 9:11
Mt 20:28
Mt 26:28
Mr 10:45
Mr 14:24
Lu 22:20
Jn 19:34
e Job 3:19
Mt 26:29
Mr 14:25
Lu 22:18
f De 4:2

---

2 According the best ancient mss.; subsequent mss. read, *a disciple is not above the teacher, nor a slave above his master*; certain late mss. omit verse 22

A fresh commandment

also love one another.^g

29 "By this, all will know that you are my disciples, if you might have love among yourselves.^h

30 ³["This is my commandment — that you love one another, just as I have loved you.ⁱ

31 "Greater love than this no one has, that one might lay down his life for his friends.^j

32 "You are my friends, if you do what I command you.^k

33 "No longer do I call you slaves,^l for the slave does not know what his master is doing. But I have called you friends, for all things which I heard from my Father,^m I have made known to you.ⁿ

34 "You did not choose me, but I chose you, and appointed you,^o that you might ⁴go away, and *that* you might bear fruit, and *that* your fruit might endure.^p

35 "This I command you, that you love one another."^q]

36 And having said these things, Jesus was troubled in spirit.^r

37 And as they were eating, he said to them, "Truly

---

g Jn 13:34
h Jn 13:35
i Jn 15:12
j Ge 22:2,8
  Job 29:13
  Mic 6:6,7
  Zep 1:7
  Zec 12:10
  Mt 20:28
  Mr 10:45
  Jn 1:36
  Jn 8:35,36
  Jn 10:11
  Jn 15:13
k Jn 15:14
l Le 25:55
  Isa 44:21
  Jn 8:33
m Eze 12:28
  Am 3:2
n Jn 8:32
  Jn 15:15
o Mr 3:14
  Lu 6:13
p Jn 15:16
q De 12:32
  Jn 15:17
r Jn 13:21

---

3 Verses 30-35 are not found in the best ancient mss.
4 Or, *depart*

Jesus honors Judas with the morsel

I say to you, that one of you will hand me over."[s]

38 The disciples were looking at one another, at a loss *to know* of whom he was speaking.[t]

39 Now there was one of his disciples reclining upon Jesus' bosom, whom Jesus loved.[u]

40 Therefore Simon nodded to him, to ask *him* whom it was he was speaking about.[v]

41 And so, having leaned in this way upon Jesus' bosom, he said to him, "Rabbi, who is it?"[w]

42 Then Jesus answered him, saying, "It is he to whom I, having dipped the morsel, will also give it." Then he took the morsel, and — having dipped *it* himself — he gave it to [5]him.[x]

43 And then, after *giving him* the morsel, Jesus said to him, "What you do, do swiftly."[y]

44 But this, none of those reclining at table knew to what *end* he said *this* to him.[z]

45 For some thought, because he had the money bag, that Jesus was saying to him, "Buy what *things* we have need of for the feast", or that he should give something to the poor.[a]

46 Then, having received the morsel, he went out

---
5 Certain later mss. read, *Judas*

[s] Mt 26:21
Mr 14:18
Jn 13:21
[t] Mt 26:22
Mr 14:19
Jn 13:22
[u] Pr 18:24
Jn 13:23
[v] Jn 13:24
[w] Ps 41:9
Ps 55:13
Lu 18:31
Jn 13:25
[x] Jn 13:26
[y] Jn 13:27
[z] Jn 13:28
[a] De 15:11
Jn 13:29

immediately, even though it was night.[b]

47 And he said to them, "When I sent you forth without purse and bag and sandals, did you lack anything?" And they said, "Nothing."[c]

48 And he said to them, "But now, let the *one* who has a purse pick it up, and likewise a bag. And the *one* who does not have, let him sell his cloak, and buy a dagger.[d]

49 "For I say to you, that this which has been written must be accomplished in me — AND WITH THE LAWLESS HE WAS RECKONED[e] — for the *word* concerning me has an [6]end."[f]

50 But they said, "Master, behold, here *are* two daggers." And he said to them, "It is enough."[g]

---

b *Jn* 13:30
c *Lu* 22:35
d *Lu* 22:36
e *Isa* 53:12
f *Ps* 40:7
  Lu 22:37
g *Lu* 22:38

---

6 Or, *fulfillment; purpose*

Chapter 15

AND having sung hymns, they went out to the Mount of Olives.[a]

2 And Jesus said to them, "All of you will be made to stumble, for it has been written, 'I WILL STRIKE THE SHEPHERD, AND THE SHEEP WILL BE THOROUGHLY SCATTERED.'[b]

3 "Nevertheless, after being raised up, I will go before you into Galilee."[c]

4 And they answered, saying to him, "Where, Master?" And he said to them, "Where the corpse is, there the vultures will be gathered together."[d]

5 But Simon said to him, "Even if they all will be made to stumble, nevertheless I *will* not."[e]

6 But Jesus answered, saying to him, "Where I go, you are not able to follow now;[f] but you will follow later."[g]

7 And he said to him, "Master, why am I not able to

[a] Mt 26:30
Mr 14:26
Lu 22:39
[b] Zec 13:7
Mt 26:31
Mr 14:27
[c] Mt 26:32
Mr 14:28
Mr 16:7
[d] De 28:26
Job 39:26-30
Isa 14:13
Jer 7:33
Jer 16:4
Jer 19:7
Eze 32:3-6
Eze 39:17,19
Mt 24:28
Mt 28:16
Lu 17:37
[e] Pr 27:1
Mt 26:33
Mr 14:29
[f] Mr 14:50
[g] Jer 34:18,20
Mt 26:32
Mt 28:16
Lu 17:37
Jn 13:36

15   Jesus prays in the garden of Gethsemane

follow you just now? I will lay down my life for you!"[h]

8   And Jesus said to him, "You will lay down your life for me? Truly I say to you, not a cock will crow, until you have utterly disowned me three times."[i]

9   But he said vehemently, "*Even* if it be necessary for me to die with you, I will never disown you!" And in like manner, they all spoke as well.[j]

10   And they came to a place by the name of Gethsemane, and he said to his disciples, "Sit down here, while I pray."[k]

11   And he took Simon and James and John with him, and he began to be deeply grieved and distressed.[l]

12   And he said to them, "My soul is overwhelmed with sorrow, to the point of death.[m] Wait here and stay awake with me."[n]

13   And having gone forward a little *ways*, he fell upon the earth and prayed that, if it were possible, the hour might pass by, away from him.[o]

14   And he said, "Abba! Father![p] All things are possible for You. Remove this cup from me. But not what I will, but what You *will*."[q]

15   And he came and found them sleeping. And he

---

h   1Ki 20:11
    Lu 22:33
    Jn 13:37
    Jn 15:13
i   Mt 26:34
    Mr 14:30
    Lu 22:34
    Jn 13:38
j   Pr 20:6
    Mt 26:35
    Mr 14:31
k   Mt 26:36
    Mr 14:32
l   Mt 26:37
    Mr 14:33
m   Ps 31:9
    Jn 12:27
n   Mt 26:38
    Mr 14:34
o   Ps 54:2
    Ps 55:1,5,16
    Ps 84:12
    Mt 26:39
    Mr 14:35
    Lu 22:41
p   Ge 22:7
    Ex 4:22
    Ps 89:26
q   Ps 28:2,6,8
    Ps 34:4,6,19
    Ps 55:18,22
    Ps 86:1-7,16
    Mic 7:7
    Mt 7:9-11
    Mt 26:39
    Mr 14:36
    Lu 22:42
    Jn 14:30,31

Judas comes with the crowd to seize Jesus 15

said to Simon, "Are you sleeping? Were you not able to stay awake one hour?"[r]

16 "Be vigilant, and pray that you might not come into temptation!"[1][s]

17 And having gone away again for *a* second *time*, he prayed, saying, "My Father, if it not be possible for this *cup* to pass by, except I drink it, Your will be done."[t]

18 And having come again, he found them sleeping, for their eyes were heavy.[u]

19 And having left them, having gone away again, for *the* third *time* he prayed, having said the same utterance again.[v]

20 Then he came to the disciples and said to them, "At least you are sleeping, and taking your rest."[2][w]

21 "Wake up! Let us be led away. Behold, he who hands me over has come near."[x]

22 And at that moment, even as he was speaking of him, behold,[3] one of the twelve approached; and with him a crowd with daggers and clubs, from the chief

---

[r] Mt 26:40
Mr 14:37
Lu 22:45
[s] Mt 26:41
Mr 14:38
Lu 22:46
[t] Ps 5:1,4
Ps 17:6
Ps 77:1,2
Ps 105:8,14,15
Ps 106:44,45
Ps 109:21,22
Ps 145:18,19
Isa 45:17,19,21
Isa 51:21,22
Jer 29:12,13
Joe 2:32
Mt 26:42
Mr 14:39
[u] Mt 26:43
Mr 14:40
[v] Ps 9:10
Ps 20:6,9
Ps 31:2,4
Ps 37:5,7
Ps 141:1,8,9
Ps 142:1-7
Mt 26:44
[w] Mt 26:45
Mr 14:41
[x] Joe 1:5
Mt 26:46
Mr 14:42
Jn 18:2

---

1 Certain later mss. add, *For the spirit is willing, but the flesh is weak*
2 Certain later mss. add, *The hour has come – behold, the son of man is handed over, into the hands of sinners*
3 Certain later mss. add, *Judas*

The Gospel of Jesus of Nazareth

Jesus is seized

priests and the scribes and the elders.^y

23 Now he who was handing him over had given an indication, saying to them, "Whomever I kiss, is he. Lay hold of him, and lead *him* away safely."^z

24 And immediately, having come up to Jesus, he said, "Rejoice, Rabbi!" – and he kissed him.^a

25 But Jesus said to him, "Friend, for whom have you come?"^b

26 ⁴[Then Jesus, knowing all the things that were coming to him, came forth and said to them, "Whom do you seek?"^c

27 They answered him, "Jesus of Nazareth." He said to them, "I AM."^d

28 Therefore, as soon as he said to them, "I AM", they drew back among the *trees* and fell on the ground.^e

29 Therefore he asked them again, "Whom do you seek?" And they said, "Jesus of Nazareth."^f

30 Jesus answered, "I said to you, I AM. Therefore, if you seek me, permit these *others* to go away."^g]

31 Then, having approached, they threw *their* hands upon Jesus and laid hold of him.^h

32 But those around him, having seen what was

---
4 Verses 26-30 are not found in the best ancient mss.

y Mt 26:47
  Mr 14:43
  Lu 22:47
  Jn 18:3
z Mt 26:48
  Mr 14:44
  Lu 22:47
a Pr 24:26
  Mt 26:49
  Mr 14:45
b Mt 26:50
c Jn 18:4
d Ex 3:14
  Jn 18:5
e Jn 18:6
f Jn 18:7
g Jn 18:8
h Mt 26:50
  Mr 14:46

The disciples flee, leaving Jesus behind

going to happen, said, "Master, if we will strike with the dagger?"[i]

33 Then [5]Simon the Zealous drew *his* dagger and struck the high priest's slave, and cut off his ear;[j] and the slave's name was Malchus.[k]

34 Then Jesus said to him, "Put your dagger away in its place.[l] The cup which my Father has given me, will I not drink it?[m]

35 "How *else* then might the Scriptures be fulfilled, since it must come about in this way?"[n]

36 And having answered, Jesus said to them, "As against a robber, have you come out with daggers and clubs to apprehend me?[o]

37 "Every day I was with you in the temple, teaching, and you did not lay hold of me, but that the Scriptures might be fulfilled."[p]

38 And having left him *behind*, they all fled.[q]

39 And a certain young man was following along with him, having thrown a linen cloth about *his* naked *body*, and they laid hold of him.[r]

40 But the *young man*, having left the linen cloth behind, fled naked.[s]

---

i Lu 22:49
j Ex 21:6
   De 15:17
   Mt 26:51
   Mr 14:47
   Lu 22:50
k Jn 18:10
l Mt 26:52
m Jer 25:28
   Jn 18:11
n Mt 26:54
o Mt 26:55
   Mr 14:48
   Lu 22:52
p Mt 26:55,56
   Mr 14:49
   Lu 22:53
q Pr 24:10,11
   Mt 26:56
   Mr 14:50
r Mr 14:51
s Mr 14:52

---

5 According to the best ancient mss.; most later mss. read, *a certain one of them*

The Gospel of Jesus of Nazareth

15   Simon is questioned by those standing in the courtyard

_t *Lu 22:54*
_u *Mt 26:47*
   Mr 14:43
_v *Mt 26:14*
   Mr 14:10
   Lu 22:3,4
_w *Jn 18:15*
_x *Jn 18:16*
_y *Mr 14:54*
   Lu 22:55
   Jn 18:18
_z *Mr 14:66*
_a *Mt 26:69*
   Mr 14:67
   Lu 22:56
   Jn 18:17
_b *Mt 26:70*
   Lu 22:57
   Jn 18:17
_c *Mr 14:68*

41 And having apprehended him, they led him away and brought him into the high priest's house.[t]

42 And Simon and the other disciple[u] were following Jesus; but that disciple was known to the high priest,[v] and he entered with Jesus into the courtyard of the high priest.[w]

43 But Simon stood at the door outside. Therefore the other disciple, who was known to the high priest, went out and spoke to the doorkeeper, and brought Simon in.[x]

44 But the slaves and the attendants were standing there, having made a heap of burning coals, since it was cold, and they were warming themselves. And Simon was standing with them, and warming himself.[y]

45 And Simon was below, in the courtyard; and one the high priest's slave-girls came,[z]

46 and having seen Simon warming himself, and having peered at him, *she* said *to him,* "You also were with Jesus, the Galilean."[a]

47 But he denied *it* before *them* all, saying, "I do not know what you are saying."[b] And he went out to the porch.[c]

Simon denies Jesus three times

48 And the slave-girl, having seen him, again began to say to those standing by, "This *fellow* is one of them."[d]

49 And again he denied *it* with an oath – "Since I do not know the man!"[e]

50 But after a little *while*, those who stood *there*, having come near, said to Simon, "Truly, you also are from them, for even your speech makes you plainly clear."[f]

51 But he began to curse, and to swear, "I do not know this man of whom you speak!" And immediately a cock crowed.[g]

52 And Simon remembered Jesus' statement, he having said to him, "Before a cock crows, you will deny me three times." And having gone out, he wept bitterly.[h]

d Mt 26:71
  Mr 14:69
  Lu 22:58
  Jn 18:25
e Mt 26:72
  Mr 14:70
  Lu 22:58
  Jn 18:25
f Mt 26:73
  Mr 14:70
  Lu 22:59
  Jn 18:26
g Mt 26:74
  Mr 14:71
  Lu 22:60
  Jn 18:27
h Mt 26:75
  Mr 14:72
  Lu 22:61,62

Chapter 16

AND when it became day, the council of the elders of the people, both the chief priests and the scribes, were gathered together, and they led him away into their ¹Sanhedrin.ᵃ

2 And the chief priests and all the ¹Sanhedrin sought evidence against Jesus, but did not find *any*.ᵇ

3 For many ²were bearing witness against him, but the testimonies were not ³equal.ᶜ

4 But some *other witnesses*,ᵈ having come forward, were bearing false witness against him, saying,ᵉ

5 "Since we heard him saying, 'I will overthrow this temple,ᶠ the *one* made with hands, and in three days I will build another, not made by hands.'" ᵍ

6 And not even in this manner was their evidence ³equal.ʰ

---

1 Gr. *synedrion*; lit., *a sitting together*
2 Certain later mss. read, *were bearing false witness*
3 Or, *consistent*

Margin references

a Lu 22:66
b Ex 12:3
   Le 22:20
   Job 31:6
   Mr 14:55
c De 19:15
   Mr 14:56
d De 19:15
e Ps 27:12-14
   Ps 35:11,12
   Mt 26:60
   Mr 14:57
f Mt 24:2
   Mr 13:2
   Lu 21:6
g Ps 109:1-5
   Pr 12:17
   Mt 26:61
   Mr 14:58
h Ex 23:1
   De 19:16-19
   Mr 14:59

Jesus blasphemes before the Sanhedrin 16

7   And the high priest, having stood up in the midst *of the proceedings*, questioned Jesus, saying, "Do you not answer, not even one *thing, to* what these witnesses give *as* evidence against you?"[i]

8   But he was silent, and did not answer, not one *thing*.[j] Again the high priest was questioning him, and said to him, "Are you the [4]messiah, the son of the Blessed *One*?"[k]

9   And Jesus said, [5]"I AM."[l]

10   But the high priest, having torn his robes, said, "What need have we any more of witnesses?"[m]

11   "You heard the blasphemy!"[n] How does it seem to you?" And they all condemned him *as* liable, to be *put to* death.[o]

12   And some began to spit on him,[p] and to cover up his face and to strike him with their fists,[q] and to say to him, "Prophesy!"[r] And *with* blows the attendants took hold of him.[s]

[i] Mt 26:62
Mr 14:60
Jn 7:51
[j] Ps 17:3
Ps 39:9
Isa 53:6,7,10
[k] De 17:15
2Sa 7:12-16
1Ch 17:11-14
1Ch 28:4-7
Ps 2:7
Ps 89:20,26,27
Mt 26:63
Mr 14:61
Lu 22:70
[l] Ex 3:14
Ex 6:2,3
Mr 14:62
Lu 22:70
[m] Mt 26:65
Mr 14:63
Lu 22:71
[n] Ex 20:7
[o] Le 24:16
De 17:6
Ps 109:7
Mt 26:66
Mr 14:64
[p] Job 30:10
[q] Isa 50:6
[r] De 18:22
[s] Eze 7:9
Mt 26:67
Mr 14:65

---

4 Gr., *messias*, for the Hebrew *mashiach*; certain later mss. read, *christos*
5 Lit., יהוה, or *YHWH*, and appearing thus in the best ancient mss.; the Hebrew Tetragrammaton signifies the Hebrew tribal name for God, which the Jews ceased to pronounce about 300 BCE, considering it too sacred and fearing desecration; when entering the Holy of Holies once each year on the Day of Atonement, the high priest was permitted to say aloud the sacred name, a privilege reserved to him alone; for all others, enunciation of the sacred name was judged blasphemous; certain mss. read, ΙΑΩ ; certain mss. read, ΠΙΠΙ ; most later mss. read, Ἐγώ εἰμι, or, *I am*

Jesus is handed over to Pilate

t Mt 27:1
   Mr 15:1
u Mt 27:2
   Mr 15:1
   Lu 23:1
v Mt 27:3
w Mt 26:39
   Mr 14:36
   Lu 22:42
x Mt 27:4
y Ge 2:6,7
   Isa 64:8
   Zec 11:13
z Isa 29:16
   Mt 27:5
a Jn 18:28
b Jn 18:29

13 Now, morning having come, the chief priests and the elders of the people all took counsel against Jesus, so that they might put him to death;[t]

14 and having bound him, they led *him* away and handed him over to [6]Pilate, the governor.[u]

15 Then [7]the *one* having handed him over, having seen that he was condemned, returned the thirty silver coins to the chief priests and elders,[v]

16 saying, "[8]I am guiltless of this *man's* blood.[w] You will see!" But they said, "What *is that* to us? You will see!"[x]

17 And having thrown the silver coins into the temple,[y] he withdrew.[z]

18 Then they led Jesus from Caiaphas into the [9]Praetorium. Now it was early, and they did not enter into the Praetorium, that they might not be defiled, but might eat the Passover.[a]

19 Therefore Pilate went out to them, and said, "What accusation do you bring against this man?"[b]

20 And they answered, saying to him, "If he were

---

6 The cognomen of Pontius Pilate, the Roman prefect of Judea from 26–36 CE
7 Certain later mss. add, *Judas*
8 According to the best ancient mss.; certain later mss. read, *I have sinned, having handed over innocent blood*
9 The official residence, or palace, of the governor

The Gospel of Jesus of Nazareth

Pilate questions Jesus

not evil, we would not have handed him over to you."[c]

21 But they began to accuse him, saying, "We found this *man* perverting our nation, and forbidding to give tribute to Caesar, and saying *he* himself is [10]Christ, a king."[d]

22 Therefore Pilate went again into the Praetorium and summoned Jesus, and said to him, "Are you the king of the Jews?"[e]

23 And Jesus answered, "Do you say this from yourself, or did others say *it* to you about me?"[f]

24 And Pilate answered, "I am not a Jew. Your nation, and the chief priests, handed you over to me. What did you do?"[g]

25 And Jesus answered, "My kingdom is not of this world. If my kingdom were of this world, my attendants would be striving that I might not be handed over now *by* the Jews. But my kingdom is not from this source."[h]

26 Therefore Pilate said to him, "So then, you are a king?" And Jesus answered, "You say that I am a king.[i]

27 "I have been born into this,[j] and for this I have come into the world, that I might bear witness to the

[c] Le 24:16
De 13:1-5
Jn 18:30
[d] Ps 109:2-5
Lu 23:2
[e] Mt 27:11
Mr 15:2
Lu 23:3
Jn 18:33
[f] Jn 18:34
[g] Jn 18:35
[h] Jn 18:36
[i] Mt 27:11
Mr 15:2
Lu 23:3
Jn 18:37
[j] Nu 27:16,17
Zec 13:7
Mt 9:36
Jn 10:11

---
10 Gr. *christon*; lit., *the anointed one*

The Gospel of Jesus of Nazareth

truth. Everyone who is of the truth, hears my voice."^k

28 And Pilate said to him, "What is truth?" And having said this, he went out again to the Jews and said to them, "I find not one fault in him."^l

29 But they were insisting, saying, "He stirs up the people, teaching throughout all of Judea, and has started *in* Galilee *before coming* as far as here."^m

30 But having heard *this*, Pilate asked if the man were a Galilean;^n and having realized that he was from Herod's jurisdiction, he sent him up to Herod, who was himself also in Jerusalem in those days.^o

31 And Herod, having seen Jesus, rejoiced greatly, for he had been wanting to see him for a long time, on account of what he was hearing about him; and he was hoping to see some sign done by him.^p

32 And he questioned him with many words, but he answered him not one.^q

33 And the chief priests and the scribes had stood by, accusing him vehemently.^r

34 But having disdained him — and Herod together with his troops having mocked *him*, and having thrown a brilliant robe about *him* — he sent him *back* up to Pilate.^s

---

k De 29:4
  Jn 8:31,32
  Jn 8:43
  Jn 18:37
l Lu 23:4
  Jn 18:38
m Lu 23:5
n Lu 23:6
o Lu 23:7
p Lu 23:8
q Ps 39:9
  Lu 23:9
r Ps 38:19,20
  Lu 23:10
s Lu 23:11

The chief priests object to Jesus being released

35 Now Pilate, having called together the chief priests and the rulers and the people,[t]

36 said to them, "You brought this man to me, as *the cause of* the people turning away; and behold, having examined him before you, I have found not one fault in this man, against whom you make accusation.[u]

37 "But neither *did* Herod, for he sent him *back* up to us; and behold, nothing worthy of death is done by him.[v]

38 "Therefore, having chastised him, I will release him."[w]

39 But the Jews answered him, saying, "We have a law, and according to the law, he ought to die,[x] since he made himself a son of God."[y]

40 Therefore Pilate said to them, "Take him yourselves, and judge him according to your law." But they said to him, "It is not permitted to us to put anyone to death."[z]

41 And as he was sitting upon the tribunal, his wife sent *word* to him, saying, "*Let there be* nothing *between* you and that righteous *man*, for today I suffered many *things* in a dream on account of him."[a]

42 Therefore, when Pilate heard this word, he was

---

t Lu 23:13
u Le 22:20
   Lu 23:14
v Lu 23:15
w Lu 23:16
x Ex 20:7
   Le 24:16
   De 17:12
   De 18:20
y Ge 17:10-13
   Ex 4:22
   Le 12:3
   Ps 82:6
   Lu 2:21-24
   Jn 19:7
z Nu 19:11-13
   Jn 18:28
   Jn 18:31
a Mt 27:19

Pilate again questions Jesus

rather frightened,[b]

43 and he again went into the Praetorium, and said to Jesus, "Where are you from?" But Jesus did not give him an answer.[c]

44 Then Pilate said to him, "You do not speak to me? Do you not know that I have authority to release you, and I have authority to crucify you?"[d]

45 But Jesus answered him, saying, "You would not have any authority over me, except it be given to you from above.[e] On account of this, the *one* having handed me over to you has great sin."[f]

46 From this point, Pilate was seeking to release him. But the Jews were shouting, "If you release this *man*, you are no friend of Caesar! Everyone making himself the king speaks against Caesar!"[g]

47 Therefore Pilate, having heard these words, led Jesus out and sat down upon the tribunal, at a place called the [11]Lithostrotos, but in Hebrew, Gabbath.[h]

48 And in his being accused by the chief priests and the elders, he answered not one *thing*.[i]

49 And Pilate questioned him again, saying, "Do you not answer? Not one *thing*? See how many *things*

---

[b] Jn 19:8
[c] Ps 39:9; Jn 19:9
[d] Jn 19:10
[e] Ps 22:28; Ps 47:2,7,8
[f] Mt 26:39; Mr 14:36; Lu 22:42; Jn 19:11
[g] Jn 19:12
[h] Jn 19:13
[i] Mt 27:12; Mr 15:3

11 Lit., *strewn with stone*; or, *mosaic pavement*

The crowd calls on Pilate to release Barabbas 16

they accuse you of!"^j

50 But Jesus made no further answer,^k wherefore Pilate was amazed.^l

51 Now at the feast, the governor was accustomed to release one prisoner to the crowd, whomever they wished.^m

52 And they had at that time a notable prisoner called Jesus Barabbas.^n

53 They being therefore gathered together, Pilate said to them, "Whom do you want me to release to you? Jesus Barabbas, or Jesus, whom you call the king of the Jews?"^o

54 Therefore they were shouting again, saying "Not this *man*, but Barabbas!" Now Barabbas was a robber,^p imprisoned with the fellow insurgents who had committed murder in the insurrection.^q

55 And having gone up, the crowd began to petition *him to do* according to how he did for them.^r

56 But Pilate answered them, saying, "Do you want me to release to you the king of the Jews?"^s

57 But the chief priests stirred up the crowd, that he might rather release Barabbas to them.^t

58 And again, Pilate called to them, *for he was*

j Isa 53:7
   Mr 15:4
k Mt 27:13
l Ps 38:13-15
   Mt 27:14
   Mr 15:5
m Mt 27:15
   Mr 15:6
n Mt 27:16
o Mt 27:17
   Mr 15:12
p Jn 18:40
q Mr 15:7
r Mr 15:8
s Mr 15:9
t Mt 27:20
   Mr 15:11

Pilate accedes to the crowd's demands

wishing to release Jesus.^u

59 But they were shouting, saying, "Crucify! Crucify him!"^v

60 And Pilate said to them, "For what? Did this *man* commit evil? I found in him no cause for death. Therefore, having punished him, I will release *him*." But they were shouting all the more, "Crucify him!"^w

61 But Pilate, having seen that it availed nothing, but rather that a riot was developing, having taken water, washed his hands in view of the crowd.^x

62 And Pilate passed judgment, that their request be granted.^y

63 Then he released Barabbas to them, but having scourged Jesus,^z he handed him over so that he might be crucified.^a

---

u Mt 27:21
   Mr 15:12
   Lu 23:20
v Mt 27:22
   Mr 15:13
   Lu 23:21
w Mt 27:23
   Mr 15:14
   Lu 23:22,23
x Ps 26:5,6
   Mt 27:24
y Lu 23:24
z Jn 19:1
a Ge 22:11,12
   Ps 79:11
   Mt 27:26
   Mr 15:15
   Lu 23:25

Chapter 17

Now the soldiers led him away within the courtyard, and they called together the entire cohort.[a]

2 And having stripped him, they put a crimson robe around him,[b]

3 and having woven a crown out of thorns, they put *it* on his head, and a reed in his right hand; and having fallen on their knees before him, they mocked him, saying, "Hail, king of the Jews!"[c]

4 And having spat upon him, they took the reed and beat him on his head.[d]

5 And when they had mocked him, they took the robe off him, and clothed him with his garments; and they led him away to crucify him.[e]

6 And they compelled one *who was* passing by — Simon of Cyrene, the father of Alexander and Rufus, *who was* coming from the country — that he might carry his cross.[f]

---

a Mt 27:27
   Mr 15:16
b Mt 27:28
   Mr 15:17
c 1Sa 10:24
   2Ki 11:12
   Ps 35:15-17
   Mt 27:29
   Mr 15:17-19
   Jn 19:2,3
d 2Sa 7:14
   Ps 39:10,11
   Pr 13:24
   Isa 50:6
   La 3:1
   Mt 27:30
   Mr 15:19
   Jn 19:3
e Mt 27:31
   Mr 15:20
f Mt 27:32
   Mr 15:21
   Lu 23:26

Jesus is crucified

7 And they brought him to Golgotha, a place which is called *the* place of a skull.^g

8 And they gave him wine laced with myrrh,^h but he did not take it.ⁱ

9 And crucifying him,^j they also divided his garments, casting lots for them, who should take what.^k

10 And it was the ¹third hour, and they crucified him.^l

11 Moreover, Pilate wrote an inscription *with the charge* and put it on the cross, and it was written *there*, "JESUS OF NAZARETH, THE KING OF THE JEWS."^m

12 This inscription was therefore read by many of the Jews, for the place where Jesus was crucified was near to the city, and it was written in Hebrew, Latin *and* Greek.ⁿ

13 The chief priests of the Jews therefore said to Pilate, "Do not write, 'The King of the Jews', but 'Since he said, I am the King of the Jews.'"^o

14 Pilate answered, "What I have written, I have written."^p

---

g Pr 24:11
  Mt 27:33
  Mr 15:22
  Lu 23:33
  Jn 19:17
h Pr 31:6,7
i Mt 27:34
  Mr 15:23
j Ge 22:9
  Ex 12:3,6,7
  De 16:2
  Ps 38:2
  Isa 53:5
k Ps 22:18
  Mt 27:35
  Mr 15:24
  Lu 23:34
  Jn 19:23,24
l Zec 13:7
  Mr 15:25
m De 18:15
  Job 31:35
  Jer 23:5
  Mt 27:37
  Mr 15:26
  Lu 23:38
  Jn 1:49
  Jn 19:19
n Lu 23:38
  Jn 19:20
o Jn 19:21
p Jn 19:22

1 I.e., 9 a.m.

The women beside the cross

15 And they crucified the two robbers with him,[q] one on the right, and one on his left.[r]

16 And those passing by reviled him, shaking their heads and saying,[s] "Aha! The *one* destroying the temple and raising it up in three days,[t]

17 save yourself, having come down from the cross!"[u]

18 And in like manner, the chief priests, mocking *him* among each other, with the scribes, said, "He saved others, *but* he is not able to save himself.[v]

19 "Let the King of Israel come down now from the cross, and we will believe!"[w]

20 "He trusted in God[x] – let him deliver him now if he wants him,[y] for he said, 'I am a son of God.'"[z]

21 And *with* the same *reproach*, the robbers, those having been crucified with him, reviled him *as well*.[a]

22 But beside Jesus' cross stood his mother,[b] and his mother's sister, Mary the [2]*mother* [3]of James the little and of Joses, and Mary the Magdalene.[c]

23 Therefore Jesus, having seen *his* mother, and the disciple standing by, whom he loved,[d] said to *his*

q Isa 53:12
r Mt 27:38
   Mr 15:27
   Lu 23:33
   Jn 19:18
s Ps 35:15,16
   Ps 109:25
   La 3:14,59-63
t Mt 27:39,40
   Mr 15:29
   Jn 2:19
u Mt 27:40
   Mr 15:30
v Mt 27:41
   Mr 15:31
   Lu 23:35
w Mt 27:42
   Mr 15:32
x Ps 22:7,8
   Ps 69:26
   Mt 26:39
   Mr 14:36
   Lu 22:42
y Ge 22:7-13
   Ps 3:2
z Le 25:55
   Mt 17:24-26
   Mt 27:43
a Isa 53:3
   Mt 27:44
   Mr 15:32
b Mt 12:48,49
   Mr 3:33,34
c Mr 15:40
   Jn 19:25
d Jn 13:23

---

2 The relationship is not clearly stated
3 According to the best ancient mss.; certain later mss. read, *of Clopas*

Jesus dies

mother, "Woman, behold your son!"[e]

24 Then he said to the disciple, "Behold your mother!" And from that hour, the disciple was receiving her, among *his* own.[f]

25 And it was now already about the [4]sixth hour, and darkness came over all the land, until the [5]ninth hour.[g]

26 But about the [5]ninth hour, Jesus shouted with a loud voice,[h] "Eloi, eloi, lama sabachthani?" – which is translated, "MY GOD, MY GOD, WHY HAVE YOU FORSAKEN ME?"[i]

27 After this, Jesus knowing that all things had now been accomplished, in order that the Scripture might be fulfilled, said, "I am thirsty."[j]

28 And immediately, one of them, having run and taken a sponge, and having filled *it* with sour wine and put *it* on a reed, gave *it* to him to drink.[k]

29 Therefore, when Jesus received the sour wine, he said, "It is finished."[l] And having bowed *his* head, he delivered up *his* spirit.[m]

30 Then the Jews, so that the bodies might not

---

e Jn 19:26
f Jn 19:27
g Job 30:22,23,26
Am 8:9
Mt 27:45
Mr 15:33
Lu 23:44
h 1Ki 18:27
Hab 1:2
i Ge 22:14
Ex 13:12-14
De 12:31
Job 10:7
Job 19:6,7
Job 30:20-23
Ps 18:5,6
Ps 22:1
Ps 22:4,5,19
Ps 28:1
Ps 30:8,9
Ps 69:16-18
Ps 72:12-14
Ps 88:1-18
Ps 102:1,2,19,20
Ps 106:37,38
Ps 109:21,26,27
Ps 116:3,4
Ps 119:126
Ps 143:1,7
Isa 45:15
Isa 53:10
La 3:8,55,56
Eze 28:15
Mt 27:46
Mr 15:34
j Ps 69:3
Isa 41:17
Jn 19:28
k Ps 69:20,21
Mt 27:48
Mr 15:36
Jn 19:29
l Ps 55:20
Ps 89:38,39
m Job 30:23
Mt 27:50
Mr 15:37
Lu 23:46
Jn 19:30

4 I.e., noon
5 I.e., 3 p.m.

The Jews request that their legs be broken

remain upon the cross on the Sabbath[n] — for the day *of* that Sabbath was *a* great *day*[o] — requested *of* Pilate, that their legs might be broken, and *their bodies* taken away.[p]

31 Therefore the soldiers came, and indeed, they broke the legs of the first, and of the other who had been crucified with him.[q]

32 But having come to Jesus, since they saw *that* he was already dead, they did not break his legs.[r]

33 However, one of the soldiers pierced his side with a spear,[s] and blood[t] came out immediately, and water.[u]

34 And he who has seen *this*[v] has borne witness, and his testimony is true; and that one knows, because he speaks truly, in order that you also might believe.[w]

35 For these things came to pass, in order that the Scripture might be fulfilled, "NOT ONE BONE OF IT WILL BE BROKEN."[x]

36 And again, another Scripture says, "THEY WILL LOOK ON THE ONE THEY HAVE PIERCED."[y]

37 And evening having now arrived, since it was the preparation *day*, that is, *the day* before the Sabbath,[z]

n De 21:22,23
o Le 23:6,7
p Jn 19:31
q Jn 19:32
r Jn 19:33
s La 3:13
t Ge 9:6
  Nu 35:33
  De 19:10,13
u Ps 79:2,3
  Jn 19:34
v Jn 19:26
w Jn 19:35
x Ex 12:46
  Nu 9:12
  Jn 19:36
y Ge 22:16
  Ex 34:20
  Zec 12:10
  Jn 19:37
z Mr 15:42
  Lu 23:54

17   Joseph of Arimathaea places Jesus' corpse in a tomb

a   Mt 27:57
     Mr 15:43
     Lu 23:50-52
     Jn 19:38
b   Mr 15:44
c   Mt 27:58
     Mr 15:45
d   Mt 27:59
e   De 21:23
     Isa 53:9
f   Mt 27:60
     Mr 15:46
     Lu 23:53
g   Mt 27:61
     Mr 15:47
     Lu 23:55

38 having come, Joseph of Arimathaea — an honorable councilor, and who was himself waiting for the kingdom of God — being bold, went in to Pilate and asked for Jesus' body.[a]

39 But Pilate wondered if he were already dead. And having called to the centurion, he questioned him, if he had died some time ago.[b]

40 And having known *this* from the centurion, he gave the body to Joseph.[c]

41 And having bought a linen cloth, *and* having taken him down, he wrapped him in the linen cloth[d] and laid him in a tomb,[e] which was cut out of rock; and he rolled a stone across the door of the tomb.[f]

42 But Mary the Magdalene and Mary the [6]*mother* of Joses saw where he was laid.[g]

---

6   The relationship is not clearly stated

The women come to the tomb

Chapter 18

AND the Sabbath having passed, Mary the Magdalene, and Mary the [1]*mother* of James, and Salome, bought spices in the marketplace, in order that, having come, they might anoint him.[a]

2 And very early on the first *day* of the week, they came to the tomb, the sun having risen.[b]

3 And they were saying to themselves, "Who will roll away the stone for us, out from the door of the tomb?"[c]

4 And having looked up, they saw that the stone had been rolled away, for it was exceedingly large.[d]

5 And it came to pass, as they were perplexed about this, that behold, two men[e] stood by them, in dazzling clothing.[f]

6 But having become terrified of them, and bowing *their* faces to the ground, they said to them,

---
1 The relationship is not clearly stated

[a] Mr 16:1
[b] Mr 16:2
    Lu 24:1
[c] Mr 16:3
[d] Mr 16:4
    Lu 24:2
[e] Lu 9:30,31
[f] Lu 24:4
    Jn 20:12

18   The tomb is empty   The women flee

<small>
g Ge 1:2
    Ge 2:7
    Ec 12:7
    Lu 24:5
    Jn 3:6,8
h Eze 32:3
    Lu 24:6
i Le 25:55
    Ps 49:8
    Mr 10:45
    Lu 24:7
    Jn 8:35,36
    Jn 11:50
j Mt 16:21
    Mr 8:31
    Lu 9:22
    Lu 24:8
k Mr 14:51,52
l Mr 16:5
m Mt 12:11
n Mt 28:5,6
    Mr 16:6
o De 28:26
    Ps 89:12
    Isa 14:13
    Isa 57:7
    Eze 32:3-6
    Eze 39:17,19
    Mt 24:28
    Mt 26:32
    Mt 28:7
    Mt 28:16
    Mr 14:28
    Mr 16:7
    Lu 17:37
p Mr 16:8
</small>

"Why do you seek the living among the dead?^{g}

7 "^{2}Remember how he was speaking to you, being still in Galilee,^{h}

8 saying, 'It is necessary *for* the son of man to be handed over into the hands of men, and to be crucified and ^{3}to be raised up.'"^{i}

9 And they remembered his words.^{j}

10 And having entered into the tomb, they saw a young man^k sitting on the right, clothed with a white robe; and they were greatly astonished.^{l}

11 But he said to them, "Do not be astonished. You are searching for Jesus of Nazareth, who has been crucified – he has been raised up,^{m} *and* he is not here. Behold, the place where they laid him.^{n}

12 "But go, say to his disciples, that he goes before you, into Galilee; you will see him there, as he said to you."^{o}

13 And having gone out, they fled from the tomb, for trembling and bewilderment possessed them; and they said nothing to anyone, for they were terrified.^{p}

14 And therefore they ran and came to the disciple

<small>2 Certain later mss. add, *He is not here, but has been raised up*
3 Certain later mss. add, *the third day*</small>

The women report the news to the disciples

whom Jesus loved,^q and said to him, "They have taken the master out of the tomb, and we do not know where they have laid him."^r

15 Therefore, the disciple went forth, and came to the tomb.^s

16 And he entered into the tomb, and he saw the linen cloths lying *there* —^t

17 and the face cloth, which was upon his head, was not lying with the linen cloths, but in a place by itself, having been rolled up *separately* —^u

18 and he saw and believed *them*.^v

19 And having returned from the tomb, *the women* reported all these things to the eleven and to all the others.^w

20 But it was the Magdalene — Mary — and Joanna,^x and Mary the [4]*mother* of James, and the others with them, who said these things to the disciples.^y

21 And their statements appeared as nonsense in their sight, and they disbelieved them.^z

22 [5][But Simon, having risen up, ran to the tomb; and having leaned in to look, he saw only the linen

q Jn 13:23
r Jn 20:2
s Jn 20:3
t Jn 20:5,6
u Jn 20:7
v Jn 20:8
w Mt 28:8
   Mr 16:10
   Lu 24:9
x Lu 8:2,3
y Lu 24:10
z Mr 16:11
   Lu 24:11

---
4 The relationship is not clearly stated
5 Verse 22 is not found in the best ancient mss.

18 The disciples go to the mountain in Galilee

^a Lu 4:13
Lu 24:12
^b Ps 89:12
Isa 57:7
Eze 32:3-6
Mt 28:16
Mr 14:28
Lu 17:37
^c De 8:19
De 11:16
De 30:17,18
^d Mt 28:17
Mr 11:23
^e Mt 5:17,18
Lu 18:31
^f De 33:2
Ps 50:2
Eze 1:26-28
Hab 3:4
Lu 10:18
^e Le 24:17
De 19:13,21
Isa 14:12
Re 12:9
^f Ps 103:19
Isa 66:1
^g Isa 2:2
Isa 14:13
^h Ex 16:10
Nu 10:34
Job 22:14
Ps 104:3
ⁱ Isa 14:14
Eze 28:2
^j Isa 14:15
Eze 28:8
^k Ex 19:18
Jg 5:5
2Sa 22:8
Ps 18:7
Ps 60:1,2
Ps 77:18
Ps 99:1
Isa 2:19,21
Isa 13:13
Jer 10:10
Na 1:5
^l Isa 14:16,26
Isa 23:11
Hag 2:21,22

cloths. And he went away, wondering in himself at that which had happened.^a]

23 But the ⁶disciples went into Galilee, to the mountain which Jesus had designated to them.^b

24 And having seen him, they worshipped;^c but some doubted.^d

25 Yet all these things have come to pass, so that the word of the prophets might be fulfilled —^e

26 "How you have fallen from heaven, O shining one!^f How you have been cut down to the earth.^e

27 "You said in your heart, 'I shall ascend to heaven. I shall raise my throne above the stars of God,^f and I shall reside upon the mount of assembly, in the distant northern parts.^g

28 "'Above the clouds shall I ascend,^h and I shall make myself resemble the Most High.'ⁱ

29 "But you shall be brought down to Sheol, to the darkest depth of the pit.^j

30 "And those who see you will stare at you in wonder, and say, 'Is this the man that

---

6 According to the best ancient mss.; certain late mss. add, *eleven*

Concluding prophesies 18

made the earth to tremble,^k that shook the kingdoms;^l

31 that made the world as a wilderness,^m destroying its cities;ⁿ that brought the land to ruin,^o and has slain his own people?'^p

32 "And you shall be cast down from the mountain of God,^q and destroyed;^r you shall be brought to ashes upon the earth, in the sight of all.^s

33 "And those who know you will be astonished, and you shall be no more."^t

m Ps 107:33,34
　Isa 10:23
　Isa 24:1-3
　Jer 4:26
　Zep 1:2,3,18
n Le 26:31,33
　Isa 14:17
　Isa 64:10
　Jer 9:11
　Jer 21:2-10
　Jer 25:27-29
　Jer 44:2,6
　La 4:11
　Zep 3:6
o Le 26:20,32
　De 32:22
　Isa 1:7
　Isa 13:9
　Jer 7:20
　Jer 44:22
　Eze 15:8
　Eze 33:28
p Le 26:14-33
　De 6:15
　De 7:6
　De 28:15-68
　Isa 10:21-23
　Isa 14:17,20
　Jer 12:7
　Jer 14:11,12
　Jer 15:1-3,6,7
　Jer 24:10
　La 2:20,21
　La 3:43
　Am 3:2
q Ex 24:12-18
　Ps 48:1,2
r Isa 33:1,8
　Isa 47:8-11
　Eze 28:16
　Jn 12:31
s Eze 28:18
　Eze 33:18
　Jn 16:11
t Ps 106:10
　Isa 9:13
　Isa 10:20
　Isa 63:19
　Eze 28:19
　Mr 10:45
　Jn 8:32

The Gospel of Jesus of Nazareth   127

Afterword

Is IT REASONABLE to suppose that Jesus was intending to abrogate the everlasting covenant that bound the Chosen People to their tribal God, as I advance?

For my part, and in light of the Scriptures, I cannot come to any other conclusion. Jesus' journey to Jerusalem was meant to parallel Isaac's ascension of Mount Moriah, and his crucifixion was to be the equivalent of Abraham sacrificing his son to the God of Israel. YHWH's failure to intervene — *"My God, my God, why have you forsaken me?"* — amounts to nothing less than a tacit acceptance of the sacrifice of his scriptural Son.

Some 400 years earlier, Euripides ventured to question the gods: *"For whoe'er, of mortal men, dares impious deeds, him the gods punish: how is it then just that you, who gave the laws to mortals, should yourselves transgress those laws?"* We ourselves might ask: in accepting the sacrifice of his Son, does not YHWH transgress his own Law? If the God of Israel sins in this way, shall he not be judged, and punished? Shall he not be thrown down, as Ezekiel prophesied?

AFTERWORD

As presented here, Jesus was striving to bring about Yhwh's downfall, which we may read as having been foretold in the Scriptures. Out of love for his friends, he wagered his life, hoping by his death to precipitate the end times that would lead to freedom for his coreligionists, all of whom were slaves of their tribal God. To further insure that there would be no turning back, he instigated a deliberate breach of the Law among his followers when he induced them to symbolically partake of his flesh and blood. From that moment on, his disciples were cut off from the Chosen People.

Once released from their bondage, though, what then? Would those who turned away from Yhwh be without God? Not at all — but for Jesus, God was not to found in the Hebrew Scriptures. God simply was. He neither judged mankind nor inflicted punishment, but rather blessed all, indiscriminately: *"For he makes his sun to rise on the evil and the good, and sends rain on the just and the unjust."* Moreover, there was no earthly kingdom to seek, no otherworldly paradise to aspire to. God and his kingdom were in the here and now, for the kingdom of God is within each of us.

Jesus' few other teachings would hardly fill a single page, much less a scroll or a codex.

Love your enemies.
Be compassionate.
Judge not, so that you won't be judged.

The simplicity of his message hides its revolutionary nature, for, quite simply, it does away with Yhwh altogether.

AFTERWORD

All things having been *'accomplished'* through his sacrifice, the Scriptures and the Law that had been given to Moses would pass away. Yet at the supper that would mark the beginning of the final act in both his life and his quest, Jesus left his friends with a 'fresh' commandment, one single and unique injunction that would serve as a guiding light — *"A fresh commandment I give to you, that you love one another. Just as I have loved you, you also love one another."*

This is neither a doctrine, nor a code of law, nor an ideology, but rather a simple, all-embracing precept. Love is the greatest boon we can give to one another, the greatest gift we can receive…and all we truly need.

Two thousand years after the death of the man who spoke these words, we are still being called upon to find out for ourselves where they might lead.

We have a long ways to go…

NOTES

page	source
x	Mark 14:36
xiv	Exodus 4:22
xv	John 13:23
	Leviticus 25:55
	John 8:33
xvi	Genesis 17:7
	Exodus 19:5,6
	Mark 10:45
	Mark 13:30
	Luke 21:28
xvii	Mark 13:6
129	Mark 15:34
	Lines 441-443 from Euripides' tragedy *Ion*, translated by Robert Potter
130	Matthew 5:45
	Matthew 5:44
	Luke 6:36
	Matthew 7:1
131	John 19:28
	John 13:34

ABBREVIATIONS

*Italicized reference verses point to parallel passages in the canonical Gospels.
Non-italicized reference verses indicate passages that serve to define and support
the premises advanced by the author's interpretation of the Scriptures.*

Am	Amos	Joe	Joel
Ca	Song of Solomon (Canticles)	Jon	Jonah
		Jos	Joshua
1Ch	1 Chronicles	1Ki	1 Kings
2Ch	2 Chronicles	2Ki	2 Kings
Da	Daniel	La	Lamentations
De	Deuteronomy	Le	Leviticus
Ec	Ecclesiastes	Mal	Malachi
Es	Esther	Mic	Micah
Ex	Exodus	Na	Nahum
Eze	Ezekiel	Ne	Nehemiah
Ezr	Ezra	Nu	Numbers
Ge	Genesis	Ob	Obadiah
Hab	Habakkuk	Pr	Proverbs
Hag	Haggai	Ps	Psalms
Ho	Hosea	Ru	Ruth
Isa	Isaiah	1Sa	1 Samuel
Jer	Jeremiah	2Sa	2 Samuel
Jg	Judges	Zec	Zechariah
Job	Job	Zep	Zephaniah

Act	Acts	Mr	Mark
Col	Colossians	Mt	Matthew
1Co	1 Corinthians	1Pe	1 Peter
2Co	2 Corinthians	2Pe	2 Peter
Eph	Ephesians	Phe	Philemon
Gal	Galatians	Phi	Philippians
Heb	Hebrews	Re	Revelation
Ja	James	Ro	Romans
Jn	John	1Th	1 Thessalonians
1Jn	1 John	2Th	2 Thessalonians
2Jn	2 John	1Tm	1 Timothy
3Jn	3 John	2Tm	2 Timothy
Ju	Jude	Ti	Titus
Lu	Luke		

A·B·C· EDITIONS
17840 • LA BREE • FRANCE

IMPRIME DANS LE ROYAUME-UNI PAR
INGRAM LIGHTNING SOURCE
CHAPTER HOUSE • PITFIELD • KILN FARM
MILTON KEYNES • MK11 3LW

EDITION ACHEVEE LE 1 OCTOBRE 2015
ISBN 978-2-9546352-3-1
PRIX PUBLIQUE EN FRANCE • 19,00
DEPOT LEGAL OCTOBRE 2015

www.ingramcontent.com/pod-product-compliance
Lightning Source LLC
Chambersburg PA
CBHW021146060526
44107CB00146B/1334/J